BUSINESS & ACCOUNTING FOR AUTHORS

INDIE AUTHOR GUIDES

Business & Accounting for Authors

Indie Author Guides

How to treat your writing as a business, manage your money, and use your accounting data to make better decisions.

By
Tora Moon

Lunar Alchemy Publishing

Paperback ISBN: 978-1-946132-20-8

Ebook ISBN: 978-1-946132-21-5

Audiobook ISBN: 978-1-946132-22-2

Cover and interior design: Tora Moon

To my fellow Indie authors reaching for their dreams, telling their stories, and becoming authorpreneurs.

Contents

Contents

Contents

Chapter 6
Accounting Systems

Chapter 7
Analyzing Your Business

Chapter 8
Samples & Resources

Introduction
An Author Is a Business

Treat Your Writing As a Business

Have you written or are you writing a book? It's a good idea to treat your writing career as a business from the beginning. It doesn't matter whether you plan on writing as a hobby, a secondary income, or as your primary business. It's still a business. But don't worry if you've been writing and selling books for a while, you still can apply the business basics and accounting to your business at whatever stage you're in. As the saying goes, better late than never.

In today's publishing environment, even if you're traditionally published, you need to track your income and expenses. Most authors must cover many of their own expenses, which offset the royalties they receive from the publisher.

As an independent or "indie" publisher, you are doing everything a traditional publisher does for your books. It doesn't matter if you do this gig full-time or part-time. It's still a business. You do these business activities:

- Hire editors and cover designers, and maybe even formatters and copywriters
- Pay for advertising to market your books
- Make decisions on distribution channels to use
- Determine what forms of your product to publish
- Build relationships with others within the industry

I don't consider myself "self-published." For one, I use a team of professionals to help me produce the highest quality product possible. I don't do this by myself. And for another, I'm an independent small-press publisher. My publishing company publishes books, just like any other small-press publishing company. I simply only publish one author—me. If in the future I decide it's right for my business, I can choose to publish another author's books—because I've set up a publishing company.

Even if you're writing as a hobby without a profit motivation, you're still in business. You'll be doing the same tasks necessary to produce a high-quality product, such as hiring editors and cover designers. You're probably also marketing your book so that readers can find it. In the US, if you consider your writing a hobby, you can only deduct your expenses up to the amount of income you had. You can't take a business loss; whereas, if you've set it up as a business, you can deduct your business losses against your personal income. And who knows? If your books take off, you'll be glad you already set up a business. It'll be one less thing to worry about later.

Introduction: An Author Is a Business

Who This Book is For

Whether you are Indie Published or Traditionally Published, you need to understand business basics and how to manage your money to be successful. This book will go over the various forms of business available to you (in the US) and how to set up your business. I will give you a basic system to track your business income and expenses. (Note: this is NOT a book on taxes, although I'll briefly touch on the tax aspects that will affect how you set up your business.)

You, as an author, are a business. The products you produce are books, whether they are ebooks, printed books, or audiobooks. Your business generates revenues (at least you hope it does) and incurs expenses (which they all do). At the most basic level, a business is successful if it generates more income than expenses. But how do you know what exactly those numbers are?

Through accounting. It captures your numbers and gives you a picture of how your business is doing.

Understanding business and financial basics will give you an edge over most of your competition. If you know how your business is doing, what streams of revenue are doing well—and which aren't—and what your expenses are, then you can make much more informed decisions. A look at your financial statements will tell you if you can afford to spend more money on a marketing campaign, or if you should cut back. They can tell you if you've spent too much money, or just how much you've really made.

Many people consider if they have money in their bank account, their business is making a profit. That isn't necessarily true. Just like in your personal life, you have bills that need to be paid, so too, your business may have outstanding bills and debts that need to be considered. And because of the way Amazon and the other book retailers pay, you have sold books this month, but you won't receive the funds for them for sixty-days.

Even if you're writing as a hobby, you still need to keep track of your income and expenses for paying your dreaded taxes at the end of the year.

Although much of this book is targeted to fiction authors, the principles apply to nonfiction authors as well. My intention is to make understanding your money and business as easy as possible. If you take your writing seriously and want a better chance of your business succeeding, then this book is for you.

MY BACKGROUND

Why on earth should you listen to me?

First off, I'm an author of both fiction and nonfiction. I write genre-bending fantasy books, and I currently have one epic science fantasy series published and am writing an urban fantasy series. I'm an Indie Authorpreneur (I love that term!). My publishing company is organized as a Sole-Proprietorship that I publish all my work under. As a business owner, I need to track my income and expenses to make the best financial decisions I can. I'm in the trenches every day, so to speak, living the life of a full-time author.

Secondly, I've been a Certified Public Accountant (CPA) for over twenty-eight years. Most of my accounting career was spent working with small business clients, setting up their accounting systems, doing their accounting, and preparing their financial statements. I've had an accounting practice where I worked with small publicly-traded companies. I did their accounting, worked with their financial auditors, and prepared and filed their quarterly and annual financial statements with the U.S. Securities and Exchange Commission (SEC). For three years, I served as the Chief Financial Officer (CFO) for a publicly-traded software development firm with operations in four different countries and listed on two different stock exchanges. I'm what I term, a financial accountant. The only taxes I've done for the past fifteen years are my own. Even when I did work for an accounting firm that did taxes, I did all the business clients' returns because they usually needed some accounting work done first.

With my combined experience as an Indie Publisher and an accountant, I know what an author needs to manage their money and business. I've used this expertise to help me make sense of my own writing and publishing career.

NOTE FOR INTERNATIONAL READERS

I only have experience setting up businesses in the United States. The information on forming a business and the little bit about taxes apply to the USA only. However, the business basics and accounting are the same no matter where your business is located. Some of the terms may be different, but all businesses generate income and incur expenses.

Most countries have a type of business that would correspond to those I talk about. These would be:

- a sole-proprietorship, a business owned by one person
- a partnership which would be two or more people privately owning the business
- or some type of corporation

Please check with an accountant or lawyer in your country on how to set up a business where you live. They can help you determine what form would be the best for you given the legalities and tax issues of your particular country and circumstances.

LEGAL AND TAX DISCLAIMER

This book is for educational purposes. Nothing found in it should be taken as legal or tax advice. Please consult a lawyer or tax accountant in the area where you live for the individual requirements of your state or country in setting up a business, tax requirements, and preparing your taxes.

Chapter 1
Setting Up Your Business

Type of Business

There are four types of businesses in the U.S. to choose from when considering setting up your author and independent publishing business. These are:

1. Sole-proprietorship, or more commonly known as a "DBA" or doing business as (in the UK, this is called a sole trader)
2. Partnership
3. Corporation (in the UK, this is called a Limited Company) or
4. LLC, or Limited Liability Company or Corporation

Which type of business you choose depends on your circumstances and what you want from your business. You also need to take into

7

consideration legal and tax issues for each type of business in your state or country.

Two things differentiate the various forms of business:

1. The form of ownership of the business determines how you, as the owner, are paid
2. The way each type of business is taxed in the U.S. (and I believe in other countries as well)

I highly recommend reading the book, "The Self-Publisher's Legal Handbook: Updated Guide to Protecting Your Rights and Wallet" by Helen Sedwick before deciding on what form of business to choose for your company. Because each state taxes the various business forms differently, I'd talk to a tax accountant in your area about the tax ramifications of each structure.

The various states publish the information on what you need to form each type of business and how they are taxed. Usually, it is on the Secretary of State's or the Comptroller's website.

Sole-Proprietorship

The most common—and the least expensive—form of business is the sole-proprietorship. This is a business owned by only one person. In the UK, this form of business is called a sole trader. In the US, except in very limited circumstances (which are beyond the scope of this book), a married couple must form a partnership rather than a sole-proprietorship. However, a spouse is allowed to work as an employee in the business owned by the other spouse.

This form of business is commonly known as a DBA, or "doing business as," because you are doing business under a name other than your own. In all states, if you aren't using your own name for the name of the business, you must register your business and the business name with the state or county. This is so people can check with the state to know exactly who they are doing business with. In some states, like California, they still require you to file a statement in the newspaper publicly declaring that you are now "doing business as" XYZ Company. This is where the term "DBA" comes from.

This is the easiest form of business to set up. You don't need a lawyer or any legal forms. All you need to do is check with your state, usually the Secretary of State, to find out how to register your business. For instance, in California, it's by county. In Utah, they have a one-stop on-line system. Nevada requires you to mail it in or go to the county courthouse. Each state is different.

The registration is simply filling out a form showing:

- Legal name of the owner
- Chosen business name,
- Address of the business and owner
- Type of products or services being sold
- Whether it's wholesale or retail (for authors you can choose either one, I usually choose retail)
- If you have any employees (usually none), although sole-proprietors can have employees

Then you pay the registration fee, which I've found to be under $50 in most states. When I registered my publishing company in Utah, I only paid $22 and the registration was for three years.

For taxes, in the USA, a sole-proprietorship is taxed on an individual's tax return using form, "Schedule C." Any business net income is added to your personal income, whereas any net loss is deducted.

As the owner of the business, you don't pay yourself a salary, because all the income is your own. We'll cover this in more detail in the section "Paying Yourself."

Partnership

The second form of business is a partnership (in the UK, this is a Business Partnership). This is when two or more people form a business together. A husband-wife writing team would form a partnership. If you were collaborating with another author, you'd probably want to form a partnership for that project. A partnership can be informal, with just oral agreements (not recommended) or have formal agreements drawn up by a lawyer.

Good business practices recommend a written partnership agreement detailing:

- The various duties of the partners
- Percentage share of profits, which doesn't have to be equal
- How the partnership is to be terminated
- Other considerations

Having an agreement upfront saves future trouble and arguments when there is a disagreement later. In most instances, it is highly advisable to have a lawyer specializing in business law to help draw up a partnership agreement. This will ensure all the terms relevant to your business and partnership are addressed.

As with a sole-proprietorship, if the partnership is operating under an assumed name, most states require the partnership to register and file a fictitious name statement. The information required is the same as for filing a fictitious name statement for a sole-proprietorship.

For tax purposes, the partnership files an information tax return, which reports the income and deductions of the partnership, but the partnership itself doesn't pay any taxes. Each partner receives a Schedule K-1, which reports their respective share (as per the partnership agreement) of the partnership's income and deductions. This is then reported on the individual partner's tax return. And they pay the income tax on their share of the partnership's business income.

Just like a sole-proprietorship, partners are owners of the business; and therefore, not employees. They aren't paid a salary, nor are they eligible for unemployment should they terminate the partnership. In essence, a partnership is a DBA owned by two or more people, whereas a sole-proprietorship is a DBA owned by one person.

Limited Liability Company

Another type of business entity commonly found in the independent publishing industry is a Limited Liability Company or an LLC. An LLC is a hybrid of a corporation, and either, a sole-proprietorship or partnership. It combines the pass-through taxation of a sole-proprietorship or partnership with the limited liability protection of a corporation.

Whether or not you can form an LLC depends on the state where you live and do business. Most states allow them, but there are some that do not. You can have a single-owner LLC or multiple owners. In all cases, an LLC is a separate entity, like a corporation, and has its own federal identification number. This is a more complicated form of business. If you're considering it, I highly suggest you have a lawyer form it, so you have all the required paperwork for your state. You'll also want to consult with a tax accountant, who can advise you of the best tax options for your business.

The advantage many people see in forming an LLC versus a DBA is that an LLC affords some legal protections against being sued. However, for most authors, this rarely needs to be considered. "The Self-Publisher's Legal Handbook: Updated Guide to Protecting Your Rights and Wallet" by Helen Sedwick talks about when you might need this type of protection. You might need it if you're writing a memoir or exposé. If you're just writing fiction, you probably don't need to worry about it.

Most states allow you to choose whether to tax the LLC as a pass-through entity, like a sole-proprietorship or partnership, or to tax it as a corporation (either a C-Corp or S-Corp). There are advantages and disadvantages to either way, and a tax accountant in your state can advise you which is best for your circumstances.

The US tax codes do not recognize an LLC as a taxable type of entity. How it is taxed is determined based on the underlying business structure.

Corporation

The final form of business you can choose is a corporation. This format creates a separate legal entity from yourself, providing you with some protections against lawsuits, and provides a legacy operation. Unlike with a sole-proprietorship or partnership, which automatically terminates at the death or withdrawal of an owner, a corporation is a separate entity and can continue to exist. For example, if you form a publishing company and operate it as a DBA, when you die or retire, the publishing company no longer exists. Whereas, if you formed it as a corporation, it could continue for years with your children or other people running it. This is the form the big traditional publishing houses work under.

However, a corporation is the most complicated and difficult form of business to create and run. All states require filing formal Articles of Incorporation, which creates the company. They have regulations that must be observed, such as minutes and having a board of directors. You, as the author and publisher, would now own stock of the corporation and would be an employee. You could then be terminated at the will of the corporation. It is highly recommended to talk with both a lawyer and a tax accountant before deciding on this business form.

There are two ways a corporation can be taxed:

- C-Corp
- S-Corp

A C-Corp is the default and is a regular corporation. All the profits and losses remain within the corporation and are taxed at the corporate level. Any excess revenues not needed for the operations can be distributed to the owners or shareholders as dividends, and these are taxable to the shareholders, causing a type of "double-taxation."

An S-Corp is an election the shareholders can make that allows the income to flow through the corporation and to the individual shareholders. This is commonly found in small companies, family-owned companies, and single-shareholder companies. This eliminates the double tax and gives the owners the same protections as a regular corporation. The rules governing an S-Corp aren't quite as strenuous as for a regular corporation. However, there are limits on the number and type of owners that are allowed in an S-Corp. For instance, another corporation or a foreign citizen can't be an owner of an S-Corp because the taxes are paid at the individual level.

In most instances, for a single-owner corporation or a few owners, an S-Corp is a good option.

Choosing a Name

An important consideration when deciding on forming your business is the name of the business. In most cases, as an independent publisher (or self-publisher), you'll want to use something other than your own name. For instance, my publishing company is called Lunar Alchemy Publishing Company, and it's formed as a sole-proprietorship.

Using a business name will allow you to:

- Use other pen names if you choose to write in different genres
- Have the option to become a small press and publish other author's works

In addition, it will make it easier for you to approach brick-and-mortar stores. They are much more likely to take you seriously if you present yourself as a publisher, rather than just an author. Even if you are a publisher of one author, yourself.

You can also do other things within the publishing industry under your business, such as speaking or audiobook narration.

When you set up your account with the various distributors or an aggregator, you'll use your business name—and business tax identification number—rather than your personal name. Then you can use however many pen names you want under that business name (and allowed by that platform).

One of the most important considerations when choosing a name for your business is to ensure it isn't already in use. You also don't want one that is too similar to another business in the publishing industry. Just like with titles, you don't want to confuse the consumer by having too similar a name and cover. I'd probably have trouble with using "Tora Books" or "Tora Publishing" and writing fantasy because it's way too close to Tor Books, a major traditional publishing house for fantasy.

After you have a list of possible names, do an internet search to see if they're in use or if anyone is using something similar in your industry. Then check to see if there is a trademark on that word or phrase by going to http://www.uspto.gov/trademarks-application-process/search-trademark-database. This is a free search provided by the government, but make sure it is the (dot) gov site. You don't have to trademark your business name. For one, this is costly to do. Also, your fictitious name statement filed when forming your DBA or partnership or your Articles of Incorporation protects your business name.

Your last step is to check your state directory to ensure someone else hasn't registered your chosen name. All states have this available, and the search is free.

You would do a similar process for the country where you live.

Once you've chosen a name and form of business, you'll be ready to set your business up.

SEPARATE YOUR LIFE

One of the best ways to begin treating your writing as a business is to separate your business finances from your personal accounts. I know, this can be a pain and a bit inconvenient. But it will help you think about the expenditures you are—or will be making— and ensuring they are absolutely necessary for your business. Do you really need the latest, greatest desktop computer, or would you be more productive using a laptop? Sure, the desktop might be fantastic for gaming, but that doesn't contribute to your business.

In addition, at the end of the year, when you need to do your taxes, all your business expenses will be in one place. You won't have to scrounge around for receipts or try to remember if that purchase from Target or some place else was for business expenses or personal. You won't have to worry if you make sure to pay ALL your business expenses from your business bank account or PayPal account. The stress of tax time will be much less.

As I discuss in more detail later, doing your taxes is only one of many reasons to keep track of your money and business finances. More importantly, having all your business expenses and income in one place, in your business bank account, you can more easily do your accounting—or have it done for you. Plus, you'll be able to analyze the results of your business. You'll be able to tell if you've made a profit or not and answer these types of questions:

- Are your Facebook ads profitable overall?
- How much do they contribute to your bottom line?
- How much have they cost you based on your overall sales?
- What about for each book?

Do you know the answers?

You'd know pretty quickly, if you have only used a business account to receive money in from your distributors (Amazon, Kobo, Apple, other retailers, and Draft2Digital) and to pay money out for advertising. I'll show you in Chapter 6 a few simple accounting systems to keep track of your money and tell how you're doing each month or quarter.

Knowing these things, and more, about your business will help you make better business decisions. Maybe you should pull back on your advertising or increase it. Perhaps it's time and you can afford to hire a virtual assistant. Looking at your financial statements, you may find that you are in a position where it is costing you money not to hire one.

Here's a hint I've found that works for me and other self-employed business owners who work from home. Segregate your business from your personal life by setting up a dedicated office in your home or have a separate place where you work on your writing. This has nothing to do with tracking money and everything to do with the psychology of work. If you have a work space that is dedicated to your writing, when you go there, your mind automatically turns on to "work mode" and you can be more productive. It also helps if you're a workaholic. It allows you to leave work by shutting the door to your office. Now you can rejoin your family or take care of you—you know, take a shower, eat something, go for a walk… ;)

BANKING AND PAYPAL

Whether you treat your writing as a business or as a hobby, there is going to be money coming in and going out (hopefully more of the former than the latter!). You will need a place to receive funds from the various distributors like Amazon, Kobo, Apple, and Draft2Digital. And you'll need to pay your various vendors, such as social media ads, editors, cover designers, or other people who help you in your business. There are two types of accounts you will need: a bank account and a PayPal account (or whatever is similar that is available in your country).

Your bank account will be used for most things; however, you'll want a PayPal account so you can easily pay cover designers and editors. Many of these types of vendors will only accept PayPal payments, especially if they are located outside the USA.

One benefit of paying vendors using PayPal is that PayPal falls under the category of third-party payers. This makes them responsible for sending out Form-1099s (if applicable) at the end of the year, rather than you having to do it. In chapter 4, I go over Form-1099s in more detail in the section, "Paying Contractors."

You may also want to get a business credit card to pay your business expenses. This will help keep your business and personal expenses separated for easier accounting and for filing your taxes at the end of the year.

In many instances, especially in the first few years, you'll have more money going out than coming in. If you are a DBA or an LLC, best practices are to transfer funds from your personal bank account to your business account, and THEN pay the bill from your business account. I'll talk about how to treat these types of funds in the section "Money that Isn't Income."

LEGAL PAPERWORK

Before you can open a business bank account, you need to have some legal paperwork at hand. Banks in the USA won't open a business account without the proper business filings. Most banks post the required paperwork on their website. Check this before heading to your chosen bank. For those outside the USA, there may be similar or different requirements, so please check with your bank.

Most banks require the following:

- Business formation documents received from the state:
  - Doing Business As document
  - If an LLC or Corp:
    - Articles of Incorporation
    - Declaration signed by managing director or board directors authorizing a bank account to be opened
- Tax identification number either
- Your personal social security number (SSN)
- An Employer Identification number (EIN) assigned by the IRS

EMPLOYER IDENTIFICATION NUMBER (EIN)

An EIN is a social security number assigned by the IRS to businesses. You must obtain one if you have any form of business other than a DBA. It isn't necessarily required for a DBA; you can use your personal Social Security Number (SSN). However, you'll be using this number to open many business accounts: such as Amazon, Kobo, Apple, Google Play, Amazon Affiliate program, KDP Print, IngramSpark, Draft2Digital, and Smashwords. It's much easier, and better, to use a business EIN for these accounts rather than your personal SSN.

An EIN is free from the IRS. It takes about 30 seconds to receive on-line, and the application done on Form SS-4 is easy. The application form is also used to set up your employer account for payroll taxes when, or if, you decide to hire employees later on. If you've set up your business as a DBA, and in some cases an LLC (check the rules for your state), you are NOT an employee of the business. Owners don't receive payroll checks (we'll discuss this more in the section "Paying Yourself"). In the Resouces Package available from my website, I've included a sample Form SS-4, along with instructions on how to fill it out. You can find it at toramoon.com/bizguide.

To obtain an EIN, apply on-line at: https://www.irs.gov/businesses/small-businesses-self-employed/employer-id-numbers Make sure it is IRS dot gov website. There are lookalikes that want to charge you money for this service. The IRS does this for FREE.

ISBNs

ISBN stands for "International Standard Book Number," and the best way to think of an ISBN is that it's the Social Security Number for your book. Each book and format of book needs its own identification number, just like your children need their own SSN and can't use yours. Publishers, bookstores, and even readers use ISBNs to find a book. If your book is published by a traditional press or a small press, you can skip this section, as the publisher is the one who obtains the ISBN. However, if you are Indie or self-published, then this is an important consideration as part of your business set up.

There is a huge debate in the Indie publishing community about whether purchasing and using ISBNs are necessary. I fall firmly in the camp of Yes!

An ISBN identifies the PUBLISHER of the book, not the author. This is why I believe it's important to purchase your own ISBN rather than use the free one issued by KDP Print or IngramSpark. KDP Print or IngramSpark is the *printer* of the book, NOT the *publisher*. If you use the ISBN provided by KDP, they own that ISBN, not you. When you decide later to use IngramSpark, or your local printer, or an offset printer for your print books, you'll have difficulty because you don't own the ISBN. I personally do not want KDP Print listed as the publisher of MY book. I want the freedom to choose where I print my books. It's one of the reasons why I've chosen to be an Independent Publisher rather than go the "traditional" route.

However, you need to determine for yourself if you need to purchase ISBNs or not based on your business model. They are expensive for those of us in the USA, and I sometime envy those in other countries where they receive their ISBNs for free. If you are outside of the USA, you'll need to research where you obtain your ISBNs. In the USA, there is only ONE legal source for purchasing ISBNs, and that is Bowker and their website is MyIdentifiers.com. In the United Kingdom, they are purchased from Neilson.

If your business model is to only sell ebooks via Amazon, then perhaps you don't need to go through the expense of purchasing ISBNs. You won't need them as Amazon only uses their internally assigned ASIN "Amazon Standard Identification Number" for all products, including ebooks. But, you'll need an ISBN if you sell your ebook via any of the other retailers such as Kobo, Apple, or

Barnes and Noble, even if you use an aggregator like Draft2Digital or Smashwords.

When I first started out publishing, I assigned an ISBN to my ebooks uploaded on Amazon. However, since Amazon only uses their ASIN to identify books, I've since stopped using an ISBN as it's a wasted number. I still use my own ISBNs for everything else, including my print books and audiobooks.

In considering how many ISBNs to purchase, the various ebook formats like .mobi and .epub are considered as different types of ebooks and each one needs their own ISBN. Also, each print format, such as paperback, hard cover, or large print, and each size, are different formats and each one requires an individual ISBN. An audiobook is a different format type and needs a separate ISBN.

Any changes to the title, or if you make substantive interior changes, are considered a new book, and it needs a new ISBN. As you can see, the number of ISBNs, even for just one book, quickly adds up. I decided for my publishing business to purchase a block of 100 numbers. This may sound excessive, but I've already used eighteen for one series. If I had only bought ten, I'd have had to buy additional numbers by now. As a prolific writer, you could quickly go through the 100-pack of numbers. In addition, buying 100 at a time makes the individual numbers inexpensive. They were only $5.25 each, and they are good until I use them, or until we have an apocalypse, whichever comes first. If I had purchased only ten, they would have been $29.50 each.

Reedsy has a great article detailing the pros and cons for ISBNs on their website: https://blog.reedsy.com/how-to-get-an-isbn. I recommend reading this article, looking at your business model, and determining your business goals before deciding whether to purchase ISBNs for your publishing company.

Chapter 2
Business Plan and Strategy

Your Business Plan

Many businesses use a business plan as an important tool to help them focus on and build their business. It doesn't have to be pages and pages long. A business plan can be a simple word document or even a spreadsheet that puts in writing all the pieces you need to have a successful business. You should include your:

- Writing goals - what you want your business to accomplish
- Mission statement - what values you have for your writing business
- Why you write - what's important to you in your business
- Audience - who they are and what they expect from your

type of writing

- Marketing plan - how you are going to let people know about your books
- Distribution plan - how you're going to get your book into your reader's hands
- Pricing strategy - how you're going to price your books
- Mailing list building strategy - how are you going to connect with readers and turn them into fans
- Team - who do you need to help you
- Production plan - what books or other products do you plan to produce for the current year, the next year, and the next five years
- Budget - an honest look at the costs and potential income

This chapter will cover each of these items in more detail. A companion book, Business Plan for Authors: Indie Author Guides is available to assist you in creating your business plan. In addition, a pdf template you can fill out with the questions and checklists is available on my website to download for free. You can obtain a copy at tormoon.com/bizplan.

WRITING BUSINESS GOALS

Determining why you write is one of the most fundamental and important things to consider for your business. What are your goals for your writing? We each have different reasons and goals for putting pen to paper—or fingers on keyboard or dictating—

and writing. These motives will guide and determine how you set up your writing business and what you need for it.

- Do you write because it's fun, and it's just a hobby?
- Do you have stories that won't let you rest until you write them?
- Is your goal to write full-time?
- Do you just want a secondary income?
- Are you an expert in a subject and want to share your knowledge and leverage it in your consulting practice?

Each of these goals has different needs. A person writing as a hobby only needs to keep track of the most basic expenses and income to report on their tax returns. However, if you want this to be your full-time job, you'll need a more sophisticated and complete system to determine if:

- Your ad campaigns are earning a positive return on investment (ROI)
- You've covered your production costs like editing and cover design
- You are making a profit.

Many nonfiction authors write a book to leverage their knowledge and establish their credibility for their consulting practice. If this is the case, you'll want to know how your book income stream is contributing to the rest of your business.

Beyond the basics of "knowing your why," which informs your decisions, it's always a good idea to set goals for your business and what you'd like it to be. Someone who wants a moderate living from their books is going to make different decisions than someone who is reaching for a USA Bestseller title or to make a bazillion dollars or sell a million books. Setting goals for your business is just like setting goals for yourself. If you have a definite goal for your business and put it in writing, you are more likely to do the work necessary to make that goal a reality.

Take a few minutes to think about and write down:

- Why you are writing
- What your writing goals are
- What you'd like to have happen in your business for the next year
- Where you'd like it to be in five years

Then think about what it will take to reach those goals. Include your production goals, as these are interrelated.

The number of books you can comfortably write and produce will determine your overall business goals. In the fiction space, it's difficult to make a full-time living with one book, or even half a dozen. Consider how fast you write and can produce a high-quality product. If you're only able to write one or two books a year, then your business goals need to be more modest and in line with this. If you're able to write four or five books, you can be a bit more optimistic. For the sake of all Indie authors, don't forsake quality for quantity and publish poor quality books just to get more out.

In the nonfiction space, consider if you want to build your business based on multiple books, or if you will only write one book. If you are writing a book as a marketing tool to build your consulting business, you may only need a single book.

MISSION STATEMENT

Now that you have an idea of your reasons and goals for your writing business, the next step is to think about what principles and values will guide you in your business. This comes from a mission statement.

There's a reason big businesses have one. They focus everyone involved on what is important to the business and its core values. Having one and looking at it while making a decision will inform you if your decision is in alignment with your "mission" or the values of your business. If you've stated your mission is to write intelligent thrillers that pose moral questions, you aren't going to jump off the deep end and write a paranormal romance. At least, not without considering the ramifications to your business and brand that would result from making such a drastic change.

Writing your mission statement is an exploration of who you are and what makes you happy. Really think about what type of writing business you want. Is your health such that all you can do is write part-time? Then it doesn't make any sense to have a mission statement or ambitious business plan that would require you to work sixty hours a week to achieve it.

My writing mission statement states, "I empower women by writing strong, leading women. I explore what life and humanity would be like in a world where magic exists and where the world and people are different from what is perceived as 'normal.' Sharing about the Goddess and Goddess mythology, spirituality, and lore is important to me. My stories explore other worlds and other species and the interconnectedness of life. I continually improve my writing skills and craft. I explore different types of stories and expand my creativity."

Every story I write has strong, female lead characters, has some aspect of magic in it, and includes at least one non-human sentient species. I write genre-bending fantasy and science fiction. I'm not going to write a thriller or mystery, as they don't fit in with my mission statement. This gives me guidance on what projects to work on and devote my time to, and which ones are just passing ideas. I'm constantly learning more about the publishing industry and taking classes or reading books to improve my writing skills.

Some aspects of your mission statement can change over time as you grow as an author and as your company grows, but your core values will stay the same. A good practice is to annually review your mission statement and rewrite it as necessary to reflect your current "why" for writing and goals.

WHAT DO YOU WRITE?

In the process of creating and writing your business plan for your writing, consider what type of writing you do. Are you a fiction or nonfiction author? They each have different goals and reasons for writing, and the way you market your books reflect this.

The marketing for a fiction book will focus more on building your list, author cross-promotions, newsletter advertising, Amazon marketing ads, and Facebook ads. The goal for fiction is to sell as many copies as possible and to build a readership of raving fans who will buy everything you write. Writing and producing your fiction books is your business.

Whereas, the goal for a nonfiction book is to market your services, establish your expertise, and validate your credibility. You'll gear your marketing plan more toward using your book as bonuses for your affiliate partner's programs than building a raving fan base. Your nonfiction book is part of your platform building and not the main focus of your business.

Many of the marketing and business strategies will apply to either fiction or nonfiction, while some, like affiliate marketing, usually only apply to nonfiction.

Knowing what and why you write will assist you in choosing which classes to take. For example, as a fiction author, I look at the instructor's background and make sure they've written and marketed a fiction book rather than just nonfiction. If they haven't, it's doubtful the class will meet my needs. In addition, you'll need a different type of editor and cover designer for fiction than you do nonfiction.

On the fiction side, you will need to decide what genre you're going to write in. Are you going to write in just one genre like fantasy and science fiction, which I do, or do you like to write in multiple genres? If you write multiple genres, are you going to need different pen names to keep your writing and fans separate? An author of children's fiction wouldn't have fans that crossover from their erotica stories. In fact, it would be a good thing if the readers of the children's fiction didn't know about the erotica.

On the nonfiction side, most times, the topic of your book will be related to your area of expertise. One of the goals of a nonfiction book is to increase your audience reach and gain more clients. Some nonfiction authors write about a passion they have, such as travel or fishing, and aren't looking to build their consulting practice. And others are driven to write their memoirs and share their experiences with others. A book in this sector may lead to other opportunities, like speaking engagements, teaching courses, or giving workshops.

The nice advantage of being an Indie author and publisher is you can easily write both fiction and nonfiction, if you choose.

AUDIENCE

Know your audience is a maxim authors constantly hear and for good reason. You need to know who your readers are and what they expect from your type of stories.

You'll want to get a general idea of the demographics such as age and gender. The way you will market your books will be slightly different for a teen audience versus an adult one or for men versus women. But don't obsess about nailing down the nitty-gritty. You'll want to look more at interests that span beyond the various demographic areas. This information can be valuable in trying to figure out where your audience hangs out so that your marketing can reach them.

Knowing your audience goes beyond demographics. Quite often, you are your target market. Look at the stories you read and ask yourself the following questions.

- What do you like about them?
- What do you want from them?
- What genre do you like to read?
- What themes do you like or hate?

These will give you good clues for what your audience is looking for and expect from a similar book. Write what you want to read, and chances are, there are other people who are looking for a similar story.

Another area to explore for meeting audience expectations is to study the tropes for your story's genre. Tropes aren't necessarily a bad thing. If you're an avid reader of a certain genre, then you pick up on the tropes. I love to read fantasy and all the sub-genres within fantasy. I know that one of the expected fantasy tropes is some type of magic. If it's an epic fantasy, then the story needs a quest of some kind and a hero's journey. Romance especially has tropes, and to an extent, formulas, that if you don't follow as an author you'll lose readers.

If you don't read in the genre you want to write in, you won't know the tropes for that genre. The best way to learn this is to read several books in the genre and study what the market wants. Study the books that are similar to yours. Look at not only the blurbs but the reviews too. See what readers of similar stories are saying that they like and don't like about the book. This will also give you clues in what they expect from your type of story. When reader expectations aren't met, they put the book down, write a bad review, and don't read any more of your writing. This doesn't mean not writing the story you want, but being aware of what readers are expecting. It's possible to tell the story you want AND deliver one people want to read.

In the nonfiction space, you will want to know what pain-points, frustrations, or challenges your readers have that your book addresses. Nonfiction books need to provide answers to questions or solve problems. A nonfiction book can come from the common questions or problems you see in your consulting practice or other work. Sometimes you write a nonfiction book because you see a problem and know you have the expertise or experience to provide a solution. This book came about because I kept seeing the same types of questions being asked by people on the various Facebook author groups I'm in. I knew I had the background and experience as a financial accountant to help them. I also looked at the market and there aren't many books out there that specifically address the money and accounting side of an author's business.

PRODUCTION PLAN

There is more to producing a book than just sitting down and writing the manuscript. That's simply the first—and sometimes easiest—step.

Even if you're writing only one book a year, a production plan will be valuable. If you write more, then it's something you'll be glad you created. A production plan is used to:

   a. Determine the timing when all the steps need to be done

    b. Track all the moving parts and the status

    c. Set your writing goals

    d. Decide what projects to work on

There are many steps to accomplish before your manuscript becomes a published book. Once you've written and polished the manuscript, it needs to be edited, then the changes need to be made, and proofreading done. When the manuscript is complete, and as error-free as possible, it needs to be formatted and converted from whatever word processing program you use to an .epub digital file or print ready file. This is required by the retail sites. Then your file needs to be uploaded to your desired distribution channels. (Side note: If you'll be offering your book free as part of cross-promotion or mailing list building, it's a good idea to create a .mobi file for side loading onto older kindles.)

Your work isn't done yet. Now you need to plan and execute your launch and advertising campaign. Social media graphics and ads need to be created, and the emails for both the soft and hard launch need to be written. All this before you sell one book!

The production plan will help you keep track of all these moving parts and their status. Many of your books will be in various stages. Such as, while your book is at the editors, the cover can also be in the cover designer's hands, and you can be working on the description, or writing ad copy.

When making your production plan, you need to be honest with yourself in assessing how quickly or slowly you can produce a high-quality product. It's great to set the goal of writing three or four books in a year. But if it takes you four or five months to get your manuscript ready to send to your editor, this is an unrealistic goal.

A production plan will help you set your writing goals and decide what projects to work on for the next year, two years, and even three years out. When you include which books you plan on working on for the next year or two, it helps you to focus on them. If you have a plan of action, you can work the plan; if you don't, it's easier to get sidetracked. It could become overwhelming when you consider all the story ideas you have, and if you're like most writers, you have more than you could possibly write in a lifetime.

This is where your mission statement comes in. Is that story idea for a dystopian thriller in alignment with your mission statement? If not, then now probably isn't the time to work on it. On the other hand, if the urban fantasy fits, then it might be a better choice to include in your production plan.

Will your hard-science fiction story using leading edge science take a massive amount of research? Or do you need to do quite a bit of research for the historical fiction you have in mind? These types of things will affect your production schedule, so take them into account while you're setting it up. Give yourself the time you need to research, plan, and plot your story in however as much depth as you need for your creative process.

Each author is different. Get to know yourself and your process, then plan for the time you need. The more you write and understand your process, the better you'll be able to adjust your production schedule to reflect your growth and your personality.

Your business goals and mission plan also gives you guidance in planning for the lifestyle you want. If you determined earlier that you only want to be a part-time author, then don't plan a production schedule that will require full-time effort to complete. If you want a work-life balance, be sure to add this into your production schedule. Also include in your schedule how much lead time you need to give your editor, cover designer, and proofreader so you can reserve your time with your support team.

Another thing to think about when working on your production schedule is what other products or versions of your books are you going to offer. These will need to be produced as well. Do you want to do an audiobook? If so, are you going to hire a narrator or narrate it yourself? You need to determine if you're going to have a print version, or multiple print versions such as hardcover and large print. For these, you'll need to include the time to format it, upload the files to the printers, receive a proof back, and then approve it.

Your production plan can be as simple or as detailed as you need it to be. It can be a simple list of books you plan to write with dates for the major activities to be done. You can then subdivide this into months so that you better focus your activities. For a more detailed plan, you can list each activity for each book and schedule in when to start it, how long it should take, and your goal to have it finished.

When I began writing, I just used an excel spreadsheet for my production plan. Recently, I've discovered and started using the online app, Trello. It's a Kanban-style list making app where you can make "cards" for each major task with a checklist, due dates, and status labels. I set one up for my self-editing tasks, and it kept the process moving smoothly. I could look at it and know what step I needed to focus on next.

A production plan is an evolving, changing document. You'll want to look at it frequently and update it as needed for any changes that come up or modifications that you need to make.

MARKETING PLAN

No matter if you write fiction or nonfiction, you will need to have a marketing plan in place for after you write, edit, and format your book. As much as you would like otherwise, you have to wear a marketing hat and become a good marketer if you're ever going to make writing and publishing a business.

Marketing doesn't have to be the "sleazy" sales pitches you dread doing and receiving. It's much easier to formulate a marketing plan and to execute it if you remember:

- You are offering a valuable product (your book) to your customers (audience), and
- They want to read, and they enjoy reading your book.

There are four things to consider in your marketing plan:

1. Cover design
2. Book description
3. Quality of writing
4. Avenues to market or advertise it

Your cover is the FIRST thing a prospective reader will see of your book. It and your description are your greatest marketing tools.

Whether you write fiction or nonfiction, your cover must immediately inform prospective readers of the genre, the sub-genre, and entice them to click to read your description. Study the books in your genre or market to see what is working and what you like. Because it is such an important piece of your marketing, this is one place not to skimp on costs. This isn't the place to practice your Photoshop skills if you haven't ever used a graphics design program before. A poorly done do-it-yourself cover won't sell any books. I suggest studying the archived articles in Joel Friedlander's monthly Book Cover Design Awards. Authors and designers submitted book covers, and Joel critiqued them. It helped me to understand what makes the difference between a good book cover and a great book cover. Stuart Bache's book, The Author's Guide to Cover Design, is excellent for learning what cover designers need from you to create an amazing cover.

The second marketing piece that's an integral part of your book is your book description, sometimes called a blurb or synopsis. To write an engaging and inviting description without giving away the plot is an art form. I'd much rather write a 100,000-word novel than a 200-word book description. There are many books and articles on writing book descriptions. I've listed a few in the "Reading Resources" section at the back of this book. Study the descriptions for the best-selling books in your genre and then practice writing the one for your book. You may write it a dozen or more times, and then even tweak it a few more times after you've published your book. If your ads aren't converting to sales, it could be because your book description isn't quite there yet.

Needless to say, the third piece of marketing that persuades people to buy your book or put it back on the shelf is the writing itself. You have to write a good story or provide the information promised for a nonfiction book. A professional editor can help ensure you do. Once your book description has hooked your prospective readers, most often they will click on the "look inside" or thumb through the physical book. If it looks professional and there aren't spelling, typo, or grammar errors leaping off the page, they are more likely to read the first part of your book, and hopefully, become interested enough to buy it.

Even with an editor, a few typos or missed punctuations will show up in your book. This is completely normal. You can't get it perfect, but you can try to catch as many errors as you can. A reader will forgive and overlook a few errors; they won't, however, when there are multiple errors on the same page. I've shut books and not continued to read them because the author hadn't used an editor and didn't understand how to punctuate a sentence. You don't want to give your prospective reader excuses NOT to buy your book. Some of the reasons they don't buy, like they don't care for the sub-genre or type of story, are beyond your control. However, you do have control of making sure your book is as free of grammatical and spelling errors as you can. Another advantage to Indie publishing is that when you do find any missed errors, you can fix them and re-upload your book to the retail sites quickly.

Just because you write a book, no matter how good it is, no one will read it if they don't know about it. There are millions of books on Amazon and the other retail sites, with thousands more published every day. Your masterpiece has to be found in all that clutter of titles. The only way to do this is by marketing your book. But it can't be a shotgun approach. Marketing your men's fiction thriller to twenty-something girls isn't going to work. This is where knowing your genre and the audience within that genre is valuable.

In creating your marketing plan, you need to consider what avenues are available for you to let people know about your book. Your marketing plan should include the type of ads you'll place, where you'll place them, and the cost for these.

One place to begin is looking at the numerous book newsletters like freebooksy, bargainbooksey, and the granddaddy of them all, BookBub. You'll need to research and find the ones that will accept your genre. You'll also need to look at what price they require your book to be listed at, usually free or $0.99. Search the internet for these types of sites. There are several sites that list the free and paid promo sites. Dave Chesson at Kindlepreneur has put together a nice one. You can find it here: https://kindlepreneur.com/list-sites-promote-free-amazon-books/

Many authors are having success with placing ads on Amazon through their AMS ads (Author Marketing Services). To do AMS ads, you will need tons (I mean tons!) of keywords to do these ads. Keywords here mean other authors and book titles similar to your book, as well as general keywords like fantasy. There are tools available, like Publisher Rocket, to help you find these keywords.

Placing Facebook ads has helped many authors increase their visibility and sell more books. In this case, you will need to target your audience based on interests. Not all authors, even well-known ones, are available for choosing as a target on Facebook. This can be frustrating.

In all cases with paid ads, you have to consider your budget. Determine what you can afford to spend. You'll also want to know whether the ad is providing you with a positive return on your investment (ROI). And Test! Test! Test! Test your descriptions, your ad copy, your graphics, your targeting, and keywords, to find what works for your books. And then know, at some point, your ads will stop working just because they've reached their saturation point, and you'll have to start over. Marketing isn't a once and done activity; it's a never-ending process.

Distribution

A section of your business plan should include a distribution plan for your books. As an independent publisher, you can choose the option, or have multiple options, that work best for you and your books.

The major distribution point for ebooks is Amazon for their Kindle e-readers. Let's clear this up right now. Amazon is NOT the publisher of your books. YOU are. They are simply distributors. The same is true for KDP Print. It is a printer and distributor of your books, NOT the publisher. On Amazon, you have the choice of being:

a. Exclusive and participating in their Kindle Unlimited program, or

b. Non-exclusive and listing on other retail sites like Kobo, Apple, or Barnes and Noble.

Selling your book on other retail sites, including your own website, is referred to as "going wide." (The book, *Wide for the Win* by Mark Leslie Lefebvre, is a great discussion on the pros and cons of this decision.)

You will have to decide if you want to give up certain rights to participate in Amazon's Kindle Unlimited program, also called Kindle Select. When you sign up for Kindle Select, you agree to distribute your ebook EXCLUSIVELY through Amazon. This means you can't give your book away to participate in author cross-promotions, and you can't sell your ebook on your own website. Both of these violate the terms and conditions (TOC) of Kindle Select and violating them could have your book pulled from Amazon. The benefit of giving up your exclusivity rights is having your book part of the Kindle Unlimited (KU) program. This is a subscription plan for readers where they can borrow your book and you, as the author/publisher, get paid for the pages read.

In some genres and for some books, the amount an author makes from this program more than makes up for it not being sold elsewhere. However, there are genres that don't do as well in KU. I found my books weren't getting many page reads, and when I surveyed my subscribers, 80% of them indicated they were NOT in KU. I write big, epic fantasies and genre-bending science fantasies. These types of readers like to buy and reread books. Whereas romance readers consume books at a high volume and rarely reread them. For a romance author, enrolling in Select is usually a good decision. However, you'll have to determine whether to enroll or not is right for your books.

Enrollment is for 90 days at a time. If you do find out that your books aren't doing well on KU, you can pull them once your contract period has expired. Be aware though, Amazon has it set up to automatically renew, so you have to go into your KDP (Kindle Direct Publishing) account and deselect the box for this option. For new authors and publishers, enrolling in Select is a good way to learn how to publish your books.

The Kindle Select program also allows you five days each enrollment period where you can list your book for free or set up a countdown deal. You can't do both for the same book in the same 90-day period. This is another thing to consider in the decision to go exclusive with Amazon or to go wide.

If you do decide to go wide, you can either create accounts at each of the various retail sites or go through an aggregator like Draft2Digital or Smashwords, or do both. Either option has its pros and cons, and you'll have to decide for yourself which works better for you. Some people like the control of uploading the books to each site while other people prefer to pay a small fee to upload it once and have the aggregator deal with the various sites. If you aren't exclusive with Amazon, you can even sell and distribute your book on your website. There are several options for doing this, like Selz, PayHip, or Shopify. BookFunnel has a service where they will deliver your ebook (and audiobook!) to your customer.

For a print book, there are several options. You can use a print-on-demand (POD) printer, like KDP Print or IngramSpark, or use a print shop. The advantage of using a POD printer is they only print the book when a customer orders it. If you use a print shop, it may be cheaper per book, but you'll usually have to order a minimum of 2,500 books! It's rare that a new author will sell that many books to justify the few dollars per book cost savings.

You can use both KDP Print and IngramSpark as they aren't mutually exclusive. KDP Print is the POD division of Amazon, so using this service to distribute your print books to Amazon will ensure that they never show "unavailable." Because it is owned by Amazon, few brick and mortar bookstores, even independent ones, will order your books printed by KDP Print. It would be buying from their competitor.

If you do want a chance (albeit a slim one) to sell in bookstores, you'll need to print using IngramSpark. They require your own ISBN, not the free Amazon one. The print file requirements are different. It's doubtful you can use the same cover files for both printers. They use different paper, causing the spine widths to vary. IngramSpark lists your book in their catalog, which is where most Independent book stores order through. However, they don't do any marketing. You must do that yourself.

For audiobooks, the distribution channels have opened up and are expanding in this new market. Until recently, Indie authors only had the option of using ACX/Audible on Amazon to distribute their audiobooks. Findaway Voices is one that many Indie authors are using and like. I'm just exploring this aspect of the business, and haven't used any of the services yet. Because I dislike exclusivity, I'll be using Findaway Voices. Joanna Penn's book, Audio for Authors, goes into great detail on all things audio for authors, such as getting your book narrated, or doing your own, and the various distribution channels.

PRICING STRATEGY

The next section in your business plan you need to work on is your pricing strategy. There are many strategies you can use to price your books, especially for fiction, where the goal is to make a living from book sales. You will have to try testing different ones to find what works for your books. Pricing a print book is different from an ebook because you have other cost considerations that you don't have with an ebook.

One strategy many authors are having success with for pricing ebooks is placing the first book in the series as either permafree (always free) or $0.99 (or 0.99p/0.99 EUR in the UK/Europe). Then price the rest of the books in the series at a higher amount, which depends on the genre. Having a free, or under a dollar, book available allows potential readers who have never heard of you to try your books at a nominal cost. I know I've found some of my favorite authors this way, some of whom are now quite well known. They still keep their first book in the series free or at $0.99 to introduce new readers to their work. Once a reader is hooked by reading the first book in the series, they are likely to go on to read the following books. And if you've done your job well as a writer, you now have a fan which will read everything you write.

When you use this strategy, the first book in the series is your loss leader. You won't make a profit on the book, but you will in read-through, the purchases of the other books in the series and any other series you may have. There are some in the Indie community who think authors who use this strategy are devaluing their work; when in fact, having a loss leader is a valid marketing and pricing strategy that is used by many companies for their products. For example, computer printer manufactures price their printers low and easy to buy. They make their profit from the expensive ink and toner. I have a color laser jet printer and the cost of the toner for all four cartridges is more than what the printer itself originally cost.

The next thing to consider is the price for the rest of the books in your series. There are several pieces to consider. The first thing to study is the price of similar books in your genre that your books will be selling alongside. You want to comparably price your books. This is especially important when you publish your book "wide." Examine all the platforms you'll publish on, not just Amazon. Along with this, you need to evaluate the size of your novel. If it's a short novella or a short story, readers are more likely to expect to pay a little less for it than a large novel.

The next thing to consider in setting your price is the royalty payment schedule on Amazon. Currently, Amazon's standard royalty rate is 35% of the list price, not including VAT, and it's available for all territories. There is a second royalty rate available of 70%; however, there are some restrictions to receive this rate. There is a minimum and maximum price range. In the USA, the minimum price is $2.99 with a maximum of $9.99 (UK/EUR is the same). You must select the option to distribute your book to all available territories. Amazon will deduct a delivery fee based on the size of your book from the royalty due. In addition, if you sell books in Brazil, Japan, Mexico, or India, in order to receive the 70% royalty, you have to be enrolled in Kindle Select. (See Helpful Links for the link to Amazon's pricing policies.)

All retail sites require your books to be priced the same. You can't have one price for Amazon, one for Apple, and another for Barnes and Noble. Amazon is the only one which restricts the price of your book, both the minimum and maximum. They are also the only one which has a tiered royalty structure. The only way to have a free book on Amazon is to set it free on the other retail sites and have Amazon price match it.

If you decide you want to have print books available, the cost of printing is an additional item to consider when setting the price. The calculation for print book royalties is: List price minus discount rate minus printing cost equals royalty. The number of pages and trim size of your book determines the print fee. Both POD printers have calculators that help you determine what your royalty will be based on the variables you plug in. KDP Print takes a flat 40% discount fee.

IngramSpark, on the other hand, allows you to set it. But there are industry standards you have to consider if you want your print book to be carried by a brick and mortar store. For these types of sales, it's suggested you set a minimum discount of 53%, 55% is common. IngramSpark splits the discount with the retail book store. They take a flat 15%, and the remainder goes to the store. This discount rate allows the store to also make a profit. You are selling your books wholesale to the retailer. This means your cover price is the "Manufacturers Suggested Retail Price." Book stores don't have to sell it for the price you set.

Another industry standard books stores expect to see for your books is "returns allowed." If they don't sell the books they ordered, they have the right to return them. Many Indie publishers make their books "no-returns." There are horror stories of those that have made their books returnable of being charged hundreds, if not thousands, of dollars up to a year after the sale of the books. The book-selling industry is one of the few that still maintains the right of return for wholesale purchases. This is one reason why it's extremely difficult to make a profit on print books, and have your Indie-published book carried in brick and mortar stores.

The price you have to set for your list price in order to even make a $1 profit is so high, you can't compete with the traditionally published books whose printing costs are much lower. Using KDP Print, I make less money from the sale of a print book than I do for the same ebook. For your audiobooks, Audible (through ACX) sets the price for your audiobook. Findaway Voices allows you to set your price. They give you an 80% royalty rate. For audiobook pricing, you'll need to do the same research on determining the comparable price for your audiobook in your genre or category.

BUILDING YOUR MAILING LIST

I'm sure you've heard "build your platform" or "you have to have a platform." But what exactly is one? In simple terms, it's your audience base and how they find you.

Every author needs a website. It's a brochure for your work and tells your prospective readers about you and your books. It's important for your long-term authorpreneurship to own your domain and website. This way, you'll have control of this valuable business asset. It may be more expensive to host your website rather than use a free service, but you don't have to worry about if the company changes the rules or pulls your website down.

Owning your domain, you can use whatever hosting service that makes sense for your business. My domain is my author name rather than my first book or series. A domain based on your book or series means when you write more books and more series, you'll have to create another website for the new book or series. It will soon become a massive expense and time slog to manage all the many websites. Using your author name or a brand, such as your publishing company, will save headaches and cash. It also provides one place where readers can discover all the books and series you write.

Setting up a WordPress website is easy with all the various site builders and themes. My first author website was built with the free version of Elementor and used the Oceans theme. I've since moved to the premium theme Divi, which includes a site builder and tools to build my email list. I like the control I have over my website from building and maintaining it myself. When I decide to make a change, such as adding direct selling, I don't have to wait for my web designer to make the change for me. But you need to decide what is the correct route for you and your business.

Your website may or may not have a blog. Blogs are almost a necessity for nonfiction authors. It's one way for you to establish your credibility and authority on your topic. For a fiction author, they aren't as required. Although, I found I had to have a blog to sign-up for an Amazon Affiliate account to use the affiliate links for tracking advertising effectiveness. Your website is also where you can gain subscribers to your mailing list.

Mailing lists are required for both types of authors. It is one of your best marketing tools to inform your audience of new releases, new programs, sales, etc. It also helps your readers get to know you. When you know a person—or feel like you do—you are more likely to trust that person and buy from them.

The most important thing about a mailing list is that YOU own it, not Amazon or another retailer. For example, Amazon could decide you violated their TOCs for some reason and pull your books. If you don't have a mailing list, you can't tell your readers where else to find your books.

Your mailing list is where you will find your advance readers (aka ARC team) to gather early reviews for your books, create a street team, or find beta readers. A mailing list can mean the difference between a book launch that fails and one that pushes you up the rankings.

Do NOT use your personal or business email service to send out newsletters. There are companies that specialize in managing your email list, autoresponders, and emails. These include MailerLite (which I use), MailChimp, ConvertKit, and others. Many have a beginning, free level you can start with, but as your list grows, you'll move into a paid model. These companies ensure you are following the anti-spam and data protection laws. Plus, you don't ever have to worry that you forgot to do a blind copy and your list receives the email addresses of everyone on your list.

These services provide you with valuable metrics such as your open rate, how many signed up for your freebie during the month, and how many clicked on your links. In addition, they provide an easy and painless method for your readers to unsubscribe from your list that you don't have to worry about maintaining.

I have found that my sales consistently increase when I issue a newsletter. Even those which are just updates on my writing or connecting with readers for a holiday. Most often, I haven't done any "selling" within the newsletter. I include a list of my books with a universal link (I use Books2Read) in every newsletter I send. This reminds my readers about my books, without pushing or screaming, "buy my book!"

You need to decide on the frequency of your newsletters. It is highly advisable to email at least once a month to remind readers that you and your books exist. Some authors only issue a newsletter when they have a new release. This is great if you're following a rapid release strategy and releasing a new book every month or six weeks. However, if you go longer than this between releases, you risk your readers will forget about you and that they signed up for your newsletter. Then, when they receive it months after they signed up, they unsubscribe with the dreaded notation of "spam." My goal is to send my newsletters weekly, such as every Thursday or Friday. Sometimes, I don't always issue one. I've found for my readers, this is a good frequency of not too often, but not too spread out. For me personally, daily emails get tiresome, and I'm likely to unsubscribe from the list quickly. I suggest you test what is the right frequency for you and your readers. Surveying your readers is a good way to receive feedback. You can include the frequency desired as a question on your survey.

To entice a person to give you their valuable email address, you have to give them something in return. On the fiction side, this is referred to as a "reader magnet." In the nonfiction world, it's called a "lead magnet." This can be anything with a perceived value you send to people who sign-up to your mailing list. Most often, it's an ebook, but it can be a map, or a special report, or an audio file. You then follow-up with a series of auto responders, also called drip campaigns, that introduce you as a person and your work.

The important thing to remember when designing your auto responders, or for that matter, sending out your newsletter, is don't be spammy and salesy. You don't want to sell, sell, sell, and push your readers or clients away. Generally, you want to send one "sales" email to every three or four regular emails. Andrea Pearson in her *"Self-Publish Strong"* series of books, goes through a well-thought out series of auto responders that I've used for my mailing list to good results.

The European Union established rules called the GDPR, that governs how you can gather names for your email list. This subject is too complicated for this book. Please do your own research and make sure your campaigns are compliant, as required, where you live.

You'll need a way to deliver your reader magnet to your subscribers. For those who sign-up via Facebook or my website, I use BookFunnel. I find them easy to use and they will help your readers download the book to whatever type of e-reader they have. I'm not a tech guru; BookFunnel has techies who can explain how to side load your book to your readers if needed.

One way to build your mailing list is to participate in author cross-promotions. Many fiction authors successfully use this method. Several authors join a promotion and offer their reader magnet to the mailing list and social media reach of the other authors. There are services which offer a forum for creating and running joint promotions, distributing the books to people who sign-up, and collecting the email addresses. These are BookFunnel, Prolific Works, Story Origin, and Book Cave. More are being added as the Indie Publishing industry matures. I've used BookFunnel and Prolific Works and had good results. You need to decide which services will reach your potential readers as they all require a fee.

You can also cross-promote your books with another author by doing newsletter swaps. In this case, you feature another author's book in your newsletter, and they will do the same for yours in their newsletter. I personally have the policy that I don't cross-promote authors that I haven't read their books. I do this as an element of my integrity that I'm only sharing books I feel are well written and would fit my reader's tastes.

A similar concept employed mostly by nonfiction authors is finding and using affiliate partners. In affiliate marketing, the other person shares information about your free webinar for your service or course to their mailing list. When a person signs up, they receive your lead magnet as a gift, and they are added to your mailing list. In many cases, especially when the affiliate partner is well-known or has a huge list, they will require that you have a sizable list as well. They want you to reciprocate by sending their offer to your mailing list.

Another way to build your mailing list is to advertise on Facebook, doing what is called lead generation. In this instance, the ad doesn't take the person to Amazon or another retail site to purchase your book. It takes them to a sign-up form to get your free ebook. For them to receive the ebook, they have to give you their email address, which adds them to your mailing list. This can be effective, but like other advertising, you have to test, test, test, to ensure you are targeting the right audience and that it's cost effective.

YOUR TEAM

Self-publishing is a misnomer. A team of people usually helps an author to publish a high-quality book. As an Indie publisher, you may do a majority of the work needed to publish your book yourself. There are some areas where you may be better off hiring someone else to do the task for you.

This section of your business plan examines the various tasks needed to produce a book. You'll determine if you have the skills to do them professionally or if it would be better to hire a contractor. I can do quite a bit myself, but I know that I'm not a graphic artist and hiring a cover designer is one of the things I insist on doing. Getting a professional edit, at least a line edit, is also another one of my personal requirements. The following are tasks you may consider hiring a contractor for:

- Editor and proof reader (if you write both fiction and nonfiction, these may be different people)
- Cover design
- Formatting; ebook and print book
- Interior book design
- Audiobook narrator and producer
- Virtual assistant to help with marketing and other tasks
- Graphic artist for ad design
- Copywriter for ad copy and to write your book description
- Financial accountant to help with the financial statements (they will usually also do the bookkeeping for you)
- Bookkeeper for data entry of your accounting information (a bookkeeper is not the same thing as a financial accountant)
- Tax accountant

BUDGETS

Now that you've considered all the parts of your business plan and the strategies you will use, the last piece to create is a budget. A budget is an honest evaluation of your potential income and the expenses necessary to generate that income.

Businesses set income targets when doing their budgets by using their best guess at what they can realistically achieve. Putting your income goals in writing helps you focus on them and work toward them rather than having some nebulous number in your head. In your first year or two, when you're building your business, it will be difficult to know how your books are going to sell. However, the exercise is worth it to have a goal you're working to achieve. A budget can help you make financial decisions, such as choosing an editor you can afford, or how much you can spend on advertising.

A budget is simply, "I have x dollars available I can spend on my business. How am I going to spend them?" The budget is how you plan to allocate the funds you have available. It helps you by looking at all the expenses and prioritizing them. Funds for an editor and cover designer may be a higher priority than paying someone to format your book.

To do a budget, consider all your business expenses and their monthly average cost. This will give you an idea of how much you need to make each month to cover your costs. Then consider your income streams and estimate how much revenue you can expect, based on your experience, from each source.

For the first year or two, this will be just best guesses. However, once your business is established, you can make more educated assumptions and work these into your budget. At the minimum, you should create a budget for the year and compare it at the end of the year to your actual income and expenses to see how you did.

When your business becomes more established, you can create a budget for each month or quarter, adjusting each month for anticipated changes such as a book launch or hiring an editor. Then compare these budgets for the same period to your actual activity.

Doing a comparison of actual versus budget at the end of the year, every month, or every quarter, informs you if you're on target of meeting your income goals or not. Using a budget in this way will help you adjust your business activities and decisions to improve your business's performance.

The rest of this book is about the money or financial health of your business and how to track the money coming in and going out.

CHAPTER 3
TRACKING YOUR MONEY

WHY TRACKING YOUR MONEY IS IMPORTANT

Every business revolves around money coming in (income or revenues) and money going out (expenses or costs). A writing business is no exception. If you want your business to succeed, it needs three things:

1. A high-quality product or service people want to buy (your book)
2. A way to connect with those people to tell them about your product (marketing)
3. Knowing if you're succeeding in selling your product and not overspending (accounting)

Accounting is for much more than just to figure out how much you owe in taxes at the end of the year. In fact, taxes are one of the last reasons for doing or having your accounting done. If you only do your accounting at the end of the year for your taxes, then you're missing out on all the valuable data that's accumulated you can use to make your business better. If you love data, then an accounting system is right up your alley.

Having a good, up-to-date accounting system will allow you to know the health of your business. Your financial statements—the income statement and balance sheet—are pictures of your business activity, and they will show you if your business is profitable or not. These documents are discussed in more detail in the sections: "Money-In, Money-Out," and "What You Own and What You Owe."

Some of the ways your accounting and financial data can help you are:

1. Examine your sales data after changing your book cover to determine if it was a good investment or not by the increase in sales.

2. Determine which books are selling better.

3. Allocate your marketing dollars to promote the better selling titles or push one that's languishing.

4. Know at a glance if you're making a profit—or not.

5. Show you if you've overspent on contracting services, buying equipment, or if you've purchased too many courses given the revenues generated.

6. See the trends in your sales and the growth of your business.

Besides saving you tax time hassles, keeping good records on an ongoing basis helps you manage your business better. As the maxim states: you can only control what you measure. Accounting provides you the method and data for you to measure and control your business.

FINANCIAL ISSUES - MONEY-IN, MONEY-OUT, AND CAPITAL

At its heart, accounting is simply a method to track the money coming in, the money going out of your business, and what's left over.

As a business owner, you want to know how much money you earned from:

- The sale of your books, other products, and services
- How much it cost you to generate those sales
- How much in general business expenses you had to pay
- How much you made or lost

All of this is reflected on what is called an income statement or a profit and loss statement.

In addition, the balance sheet gives you information on:

1. The value of the assets you own
2. How much you owe
3. The amount left over that is your equity or ownership of the business

CASH-BASIS VS ACCRUAL-BASIS

In accounting, there are two ways of keeping track of your income and expenses; the cash-basis and the accrual-basis methods. Each tracks the meaningful data, but the timing on when the income or expense is recorded is different.

To get a more accurate picture of your business, accountants advocate your financial books follow the accrual-basis, which is what Generally Accepted Accounting Principles or GAAP is based on. In accrual-basis accounting, the income and expenses are recorded when they occur, regardless of when the actual cash comes in or payment goes out. Conversely, the cash-basis method records income and expenses when the cash is received, or the payment is made, regardless of when the actual sale or expense took place.

In accounting, this means the month the income is recorded is different for the two methods. For the accrual method, the income is recorded in the month of the sale. Whereas, for cash-basis, the income wouldn't be recorded until you actually receive the royalties, 60-days later. The amount recorded is the same.

Accountants recommend the accrual method because it more accurately reflects the activity of your business in the month it occurs. It matches the revenues and expenses in the same months they are generated. Such as the marketing expenditures you made in November to generate your November sales are recorded in the same month.

In many businesses, you receive the money for the sale of your product in the same month, or within 30-days. However, the publishing industry is different. On all the retail platforms (Amazon, Kobo, Apple, Barnes & Noble, etc.), they pay you the royalties you earned 60-days after the month you sold your books. You won't receive payment for the sales you made in November until January.

This creates a mismatch in your accounting if you use the cash-basis system—and skews your data, which can lead to wrong assumptions about your business. When looking at the trends in your sales, if your financial records are on cash-basis, your timing will be off by two months.

For example, you want to decide if May versus July would be better for you to launch your next book release. Your accounting data shows May is a better month for sales, and you usually have a large dip in sales in July because of summer. You decide from this data that May is the better month to launch. However, on cash-basis, you're making a decision from the wrong data because the May income is actually for sales made in March, and July's income was for May sales. In reality, March would be the better month for you to launch your book.

If you want your financial records to match with your sales reports from Amazon and the other distributors, you will need to use the accrual-basis method. The accrual system will record your sales in the month you made them and then pick up the cash later when you receive it. On a cash-basis, your sales reports from your distributors will never match up with your accounting records.

Because of how royalties are paid, using the cash method makes it more difficult to correlate expenses and income and to make business decisions. When examining your marketing expenses to determine if they generated a profit, the expenses you paid in November are for the sales that you don't record until January.

However, for tax purposes, you want to report on the cash-basis so you're only paying taxes on the cash you've actually received. When the distributors, like Amazon, send you a Form-1099 at the end of the calendar year, it will be on a cash-basis. You can use the accrual method for your monthly reports and the cash-basis for your taxes. Hiring an accountant or using one of the popular accounting software programs available, like QuickBooks, Xero, or Zoho, makes this easy.

Cash-basis is the easier method, but you lose the advantages that come from an accrual system. On a cash-basis system, when you receive money in, you record it, regardless of when you actually sold the product. When you receive a bill, you record it when it's paid, not when the service was rendered.

Most people use cash-basis to track their personal income and expenses. They record their paycheck when they receive it, even if they did the work to make the money in a prior month. And they record their bills when the money goes out of their checking account, even if the service was provided a month or two previously.

You need to choose which method to use at the beginning when you first set up your business and then stick with it. It's a major (and costly) process to change the method of accounting later. If your future plans for your business include publishing other people's books, you'll want to use the accrual method, so you can accurately report and pay royalties owed to your authors. Whereas, you could use the cash-basis method with supplemental spreadsheets, if your business plan is to just publish your own books.

I personally use the accrual system, not only because of my past training as an accountant, but because I like having and using accurate data for my business decisions. I don't want to do any mental gymnastics to remember when a sale was made. My accounting records show me the correct data.

In Chapter 6, "Accounting Systems," I include examples of basic systems for each of these accounting methods.

WHAT TO TRACK AND RECORD KEEPING

An accounting system is a method to track the financial aspects of your business. You will need to keep records to track the money coming in from all your activities that generate income and all the money going out for expenses. I go into this in more detail in Chapter 4 "Money-In; Money-Out."

You will need some sort of system, either a set of folders and a spreadsheet or an accounting software package, to keep your records. You can start simple, and as your business grows and becomes more complex, you can move to using accounting software or hiring an accountant. One thing many business owners will say is that they wished they kept better records from the beginning. I've never heard one say having an accounting system is a waste of time or money.

The simplest method is to have an expanding file folder with pockets. You can put all your receipts, bank statements, and sales reports into it, then hand this over to your tax accountant at the end of the year. For this system, you'd need a pocket for income, one for bank statements, and several for different categories of expenses. However, this system doesn't provide you with any usable data.

The next system up is to add a spreadsheet where you list your income and expenses each month. This is better than the first, but it doesn't provide you with full data. This is the most basic cash-basis system you can use.

Even better is to use accounting software, like QuickBooks, and enter your data in it. For this system, remember the adage: garbage in-garbage out. If the system isn't set up and used properly, you may end up with unusable data. Using the information in this book, you can set up a decent system to get you started.

The best practice—and less time consuming for you when you have the funds coming in to support it—is to hire an accountant. They don't need to be on-staff. They can provide good service at a reasonable price as a consultant. You send them your data each month, they input it and do their magic, and voila, you receive financial information you can use. Even as a former CPA and financial accountant, I'm looking forward to the day I can afford to hire an accountant! I'd much rather spend my time writing than doing the books, but I know they are necessary for my business to succeed.

No matter what system you choose, you'll still need to keep your bills, receipts, credit card statements, bank statements, and sales reports. These can either be in a paper folder system or you can scan them to your computer. You need to have them accessible in case you need to refer to them later (just what did that editor charge you per word?)—or heaven forbid—you have an IRS audit. You will need to keep these records for seven years.

You will also want a system, paper or electronic, to keep all correspondence you have with any government organization such as city, state, or the IRS (or the taxing authority in your country). This way you can prove what you filed and their responses if you should need it later. In this case, it's better to have them and not ever need them than to need them and not have them.

FINANCIAL STATEMENTS

After the data has been input into whatever accounting system you use, it is summarized and consolidated into what are called financial statements, either by the software program or your accountant. There are two main, basic statements that every business owner should know how to read:

1. Income Statement or Profit and Loss Statement
2. Balance Sheet

The income statement shows you the activity of your business over a period of time, such as a month, quarter, or year-to-date. This document captures and summarizes the money coming in to your business as revenues or income, and the money going out in expenses.

The balance sheet summarizes what you own (your assets), what you owe (your liabilities), and what is left over (your capital or equity). This is shown as of a certain day, such as the end of the month, the end of the quarter, or the end of the year.

The balance sheet is a snapshot of your business as of a certain day; whereas an income statement covers a time interval. You can think of a balance sheet as a picture and an income statement as a video.

Chapter 4
Money-In, Money-Out

The Income Statement

One of the most important financial statements for your business is the Income Statement, also called a Profit and Loss Statement. Besides summarizing and reporting your income and expenses, it allows you to:

- Examine your business trends
- Analyze what is working
- Tell when expenditures are getting out of line

Just having a check register won't provide you with this type of useful information. The income statement is usually a page or two. It tells you at a glance just how much you've sold, how much it cost you in marketing and advertising, and what you've actually spent your money on. It summarizes the detailed information that was entered into the accounting system to show just the major types of revenue and expenses, or it can detail them for you. Accounting programs have the capability to produce more detailed reports from the data entered. This can include:

- List of all expenditures and the category
- Breakdown of sales between ebooks, print books, and audiobooks
- Advertising spent on Facebook ads versus AMS ads
- Amount of sales income for each book or series — for the year or over the lifetime of the books

It all depends how much detail you set up in the program and put in when you do the data entry.

I have included a sample income statement in the "Samples" section.

Money-In (Income or Revenue)

Revenue Streams

Revenue or income is defined as the money coming into your business from your business activities. Types of revenues would include book sales, merchandise sales, or speaking engagements.

As a fiction author, you will have several revenue streams from your books and related products. It's up to you if you want to track each type of revenue stream or lump them all together. I personally like to list them separately so that I can tell how much income my audiobooks or ebooks are making. At a minimum, you should separate your book income from other types of income, like speaking engagements or teaching classes.

Types of revenue you could have are:

- Ebook sales
- Print book sales
- Audiobook sales
- Website sales, if you sell directly from your website
- Speaking honorariums
- Teaching classes at writer's conferences
- Sales of writing courses
- Editing or proofreading services
- Royalties from a publisher if you're with a publishing house or a hybrid author
- Merchandise sales for related products (t-shirts, mugs, etc.)

Think beyond just selling your books via distributors like Amazon, Draft2Digital, Kobo, Apple, Barnes and Noble, and Google Play. Consider other places where you could sell your print books such as:

- On your website, (ebooks and print)
- Local book fairs
- Independent book stores in your area
- Local specialty store (if you have a niche book)
- Conventions around the topic of your book
- Craft fairs

Remember, if you are participating in the Amazon Kindle Select program (Kindle Unlimited), your ebooks are contracted to Amazon exclusivity. The ONLY place you can sell your ebooks is on Amazon.

If you have a speaking engagement, whether you write nonfiction or fiction, make sure to take a stack of books with you to sell from the "back of the room." Many writers conferences have a vendor room where you can sell your books.

With today's technology, you have several options for taking people's money who want to buy your book in these types of situations. A few examples for those in the USA and Canada are PayPal Here, Square, Shopify POS, or setting up a merchant account with your local bank.

If you write nonfiction, and writing isn't the main focus of your consulting practice or other business, then your book sales would be an additional revenue item for you.

Depending on how much information you want to analyze, you can break down your sales even further. This is where accounting software comes in handy. You can set up sub-accounts or even classes/departments for more granular tracking of your sales income. You could break it down by each type:

- Ebook
- Print
- Audiobook

In addition, you can break it down by series and/or genre if you write in more than one genre. If you have this information, then you can easily tell if a series is doing well or limping along, or if that techno-thriller you decided to write was really a good idea or not.

Accounting software can track the income source. You'd be able to see if your books are selling better on Apple or Kobo, or if you need to put more money into advertising to buyers on these channels.

In the Sample Chart of Accounts (found in the "Samples" section), I list the major types of revenue you'll likely have in your writing business.

MONEY THAT ISN'T INCOME

There are times when you receive money or make deposits to your bank account that aren't directly related to your business activities. These monies need to be accounted for differently than for sales.

Any loans you receive are considered liabilities—something you owe—and are not income. They get accounted for and shown on the balance sheet.

No matter which form of business you set up, whenever you, as the owner of the business, puts money into the business, it is an investment by you. In accounting terms, you've paid-in more capital; and therefore, now have more equity in your business. This can be in the form of:

- Cash deposited or transferred from your personal bank account to your business account.

- Paying for business expenses from your personal bank account or credit card.

Another type of money coming in that isn't income would be interest on business savings accounts, tax refunds, or anything else that isn't directly related to your business.

SALES TAX OR VAT ISSUES

As a business selling products—your books—you have one important tax issue, that of sales tax, or VAT in the UK and Europe. In most states in the USA, sales of products, whether electronic (ebooks) or tangible goods (print books, audiobooks, merchandise), are subject to collecting sales tax from the customer and remitting it to the state.

States, counties, and cities fund their activities through sales tax and property taxes; therefore, it's a big deal to them, and one if you don't do properly, will generate substantial penalties and fines. The sales tax or VAT amounts collected are not income, they are a liability. You owe them to the state. It's much less of a hassle to record them correctly when you collect the sales tax than to go back and try to figure it out later. (I've done both for clients and trying to figure it out later is time consuming, and therefore, COSTLY!)

When you use a distributor like Amazon or Draft2Digital, they are the ones selling your books to the end user. As such, they are responsible for collecting the sales tax or VAT on the sale. They are the sellers of your book (product). As long as you only sell through a distributor, you won't have to worry about sales tax.

The below discussion is about sales tax in the USA, because I don't have the direct experience working with VAT. Please consult a financial accountant in your country to determine if, and when, you may be liable for VAT in your country.

If you decide to sell your books from your website, sell them at an event, or sell merchandise, you're now subject to sales tax laws and rules.

Most website shopping cart programs will have a module for calculating and charging sales tax to the customer. There are also applications like Avalara and TaxJar that work with your shopping cart and accounting systems to calculate the appropriate sales tax to be collected. It is up to you to register with your state for a sales tax permit and account, then report and remit the sales tax you've collected to them.

Depending on how much you sell, this can be on an annual, quarterly, or monthly basis. You need to keep accurate records and send the payment in timely. In California, the penalty is 10% of the amount you owed, plus interest for each day you are late filing and paying your return. The penalties in other states are just as bad. Another reason for keeping good records is because, depending on your volume of sales, you may also be subject to having a sales tax audit done.

In the USA, it used to be that if you sold your books from your website, then you'd only be subject to your state of registration for sales tax. It was the only state where you had "nexus," a physical connection. Sales tax was calculated on where the item was sold (your location), not where the customer lived unless you had nexus in the customer's state.

However, with the Supreme Court ruling that came down in July 2018, this changed. They ruled that states could impose sales tax on internet sales made in their state, regardless if the seller had physical nexus to the state or not. This is now termed as "Economic Nexus," and uses the economic value of your sales within the state to determine if you must collect and pay sales tax for that state. It is beyond the scope of this book to go into detail for each state. In the resources are links to some great articles on Avalara about online sales tax, explaining the different types of nexus and what each state requires.

In general, most states use a trigger event, usually sales for the prior year or a certain number of transactions. The sales threshold is usually fairly high (from $100,000 - $500,000) before your online sales would fall under that state's jurisdiction. The transaction criteria is usually only 100 - 200 sales. Many of the states that use a sales dollar threshold and a transaction threshold require both conditions to be met (ie: $100,000 in sales AND 200 transactions).

Although, some states it is one or the other, once one condition is met, such as 200 transactions, it doesn't matter the dollar amount, you now need to collect and pay sales tax to that state.

As you can see, this is a complicated matter. Your best strategy as a business owner, selling online, is to track your sales by state. Then look at the states (outside your home state—you'll always owe those) for which you have multiple sales to determine when (or if) you will trigger that state's nexus rules. Your financial accountant can help you in setting up the accounts and filing the returns and taxes.

When you sell your books at a convention or craft fair, you will also need to collect sales tax on these sales. If the event is in your home state, you would just include these sales on your regular sales tax return. If you are traveling to an event outside of your home state, you'll need to check with the state to determine what you need. Many states issue temporary permits for just the event or time period you'll be in the state, and you'll pay the sales tax when the event closes. If you do only one or two events in your home state and you don't sell books on your website, you'll need to check with your state if you need a temporary permit. Also, some events that host a book fair opportunity will collect the sales and remit the sales tax for you. Check with the event to determine your sales tax responsibility. Most states expect payment of sales tax no matter how small.

If you've kept good records, then the sales tax returns are straight forward to fill out and file. However, your financial accountant is familiar with these and will be able to help you or file them for you.

MONEY-OUT

Expenses

Expenses are defined as money going out of your business to support the generation of income or just to be in business. These are broken down into three sections:

1. Cost of Sales. This is any expense directly related to generating business income. This would include such things as book printing expenses, the cost of proof copies, book cover design, editing, and copywriting. If you decide to sell merchandise, the cost of those products would go here.

2. Sales and marketing. This is usually categorized separately because they represent a large chunk of your expenses. They would include Facebook ads, AMS ads, newsletter promotions (BookBub, Freebooksy), cross-promotion costs (BookFunnel, Story Origin, Prolific Works), email provider, swag, and other giveaway expenses.

3. General and administrative expenses. These are all the other expense you incur to be in business. These would be such things as automobile expenses, business licenses, bank charges, professional development classes or courses you take, dues and subscriptions, internet charges, cell phone, and office supplies.

In the Sample Chart of Accounts (found in the "Samples" section), I list the major expenses you'll likely have in your writing business.

MONEY-OUT THAT ISN'T AN EXPENSE

Just like in income, you may have money going out of your checking account that isn't a business expense. The most common is withdrawing money to pay yourself, whether it's cash or to pay a personal bill.

If you set up your business as a sole-proprietorship (DBA) or a partnership, you don't receive a paycheck or salary from the business. Any money you pull out of the business for living expenses or to pay yourself is considered a reduction in your equity. I'll go into this in more detail in the section "Paying Yourself."

Other types of expenditures that aren't expenses are the purchase of long-term assets like computer equipment or office furniture, prepaid expenses, purchases of inventory, and accounts receivable. These are all considered assets and would be shown on your balance sheet. I go into more detail on these in the section "Assets - What You Own."

If you receive a loan or pay for items with a credit card, the payments on the loans or credit card would not be expenses.

PAYING YOURSELF

One area that confuses many new business owners and entrepreneurs is how you get paid from your business. Being your own boss is a new experience and different from working for someone else and receiving a paycheck every month.

How owners of the business are paid depends on the type of business set up and how that business is taxed. Only in limited circumstances would you be considered an employee of your business and receive a paycheck—and have payroll tax deductions. (Note: these are rules for the USA. Please check with your country for how owner-employees are handled for the type of business you choose.)

Sole-proprietorship (DBA) or Partnership

For both of these types of businesses, you are the owner, and you can't be an employee due to the way they are taxed. As a DBA and partnership, all your business income and expenses are reported on your individual tax return. Therefore, all the income belongs to you (and your partners), and you can pull it out as you see fit. Any funds that you withdraw or put into your business are considered part of your equity.

Because you are an owner, not an employee, you are responsible for both portions of your Medicare and FICA taxes, usually called self-employment taxes. As an employee, half of this tax is paid by you as a payroll deduction and the other half is paid by your employer. You are now both the employee and employer and must pay both portions. However, unlike an employee, the amount of the tax is based on your net earnings of the business rather than on your gross pay. If your business has a loss, then you wouldn't owe any self-employment taxes. Conversely, the amount you'd receive from Social Security when you retire is based on the amount you paid in and your last five years of salary.

You will also be required to make quarterly estimated tax payments to both the federal government and your state (if your state has income tax). This amount can be computed when you do your taxes and your tax accountant can provide you with the necessary forms.

Limited Liability Company (LLC)

For this type of business, it depends on the elections you made when you set it up. If it's a single-member LLC, meaning you are the only owner, or if it's a partnership, the rules for a sole-proprietorship or partnership apply. However, if you set it up as a corporation, then the rules of a corporation apply. The US tax codes do not recognize an LLC as a taxable type of entity and determines how it is taxed based on the underlying business structure.

Corporation

It depends if you elected to be taxed as an S-Corp or a C-Corp.

S-Corp

In an S-Corp, the business income and expenses are "passed-through" to the owners/shareholders. The tax return filed by the business is just an information return to report the earnings or loss. As part of the return, the business prepares and provides a Schedule K to the shareholders. This return shows what they must report on their personal tax returns.

The IRS has ruled that shareholders that substantially participate in the running of the business (i.e., a single shareholder) are employees of the corporation. They must be paid a "reasonable" salary, subject to employment taxes, before the company distributes any excess funds to the shareholders. A reasonable amount is based on the company and by what another similar company would pay the officer or the going wage for that position for your state. In the first year or two of operations, when the company may be making little or no money, the IRS has ruled that not paying a salary is reasonable.

C-Corp

In a C-Corp, you don't actually own the business; you own shares of the business. Instead of being an owner, you are considered an officer of the corporation. As such, you would be an employee. A regular corporation, or C-Corp, is considered a separate, legal entity; and therefore, files its own tax return and is responsible for paying the taxes on the company's earnings or losses.

For both types of corporations, as an employee, you will have to:

- Pay yourself a regular paycheck (you determine the frequency)
- Pay the tax withholdings to the federal and state agencies
- File quarterly and annual payroll tax returns

In this case, there is no self-employment tax because the Medicare and FICA taxes are withheld from your paycheck and the company pays its share.

PAYING CONTRACTORS

One question I see all the time at tax time in the author groups I'm in is about Form-1099s. This is the tax form for independent contractors similar to a W-2 employees receive at the end of the year. The Form-1099 shows the payments the company made to an individual sub-contractor.

In the USA, if a business pays a vendor over $600 during the year, they are required to file Form-1099s with the IRS. They must also send a copy to their vendors. Please check the IRS website to determine if this has changed since the publication of this book.

The only exception is if the vendor is a corporation or if you paid the vendor via a credit card. Debit cards and PayPal are considered forms of credit cards; therefore, any payments made to your vendors using these won't be counted in the $600 threshold. Most accounting systems like QuickBooks, Zoho, or Xero (the most popular, entry-level systems) have the capacity to track this. If you need help in filing your Form-1099s, your financial accountant can file them for you.

The other issue to consider when paying sub-contractors is making sure that they ARE contractors and not employees. Most states take this issue very seriously and impose severe fines if they determine the person was actually an employee of the business, but they were paid as a contractor.

In your writing business, this usually won't be a problem. Most of the contractors you hire will be professionals, such as editors, cover designers, copywriters, and accountants. It's clear these professionals have their own businesses. They work with other clients, set their own schedules, and do the work with little supervision on your part. Therefore, they are contractors, not employees.

One type of contractor that may be a gray area for an author is personal assistants. To meet the tests of contractor versus employee, a contractor would:

- Be given a of set tasks or projects
- They decide how they accomplish the job
- Have little to no supervision
- Have multiple clients

- Invoice you for the services provided

You wouldn't have to issue them a Form 1099 if you pay them via PayPal, or if you pay them via a credit or debit card. However, if you pay them with a check, and more than the threshold amount, you will have to issue them a 1099.

However, your personal assistant would be an employee if:

- They come into your home office
- Does multiple types of tasks for you
- You supervise and direct them in how and when they perform their task
- They only do this type of work for you (even part-time)

Whenever your business has an employee, there are certain things required of your business. You must:

- Register with your state's Employment Development Division as an employer
- Pay your employees a paycheck with tax deductions
- Remit the tax withholdings to your state and the IRS as required
- File quarterly and annual payroll tax returns

If you have to do payroll, I highly suggest hiring an accounting firm or payroll company to assist you rather than trying to do it yourself. They have the tools and expertise to do this much quicker and with less hassle. They also know all the rules and can make sure you are making the correct deductions from your employees' paychecks. I also highly discourage you from using the payroll system inside of QuickBooks, unless you are also an accountant. In my experience, it can create more problems than it solves because you don't know the employment tax rules and laws.

Chapter 5
What You Own and What You Owe

The Balance Sheet

The second important financial statement you will want to have and look at for your business is the Balance Sheet. This document shows you at a glance if your business is thriving, doing okay, or under water.

In a thriving business, the assets are more than the liabilities, meaning you have the funds to pay off everything you owe to other people, and your equity is positive. In a business that is having trouble, the liabilities are more than the assets and there is negative equity. It's called a balance sheet because the assets have to equal the liabilities and equity.

Like the income statement, a balance sheet can be simple with summarized categories, or detailed and list the various accounts within those categories. For those accounts that you want to know more detail, like what makes up prepaid expenses, your accountant or accounting program can provide you with this information with supplemental reports.

I have included a sample balance sheet in the "Samples" section.

Assets - What You Own

The first section of the balance sheet is what you own or your assets. (For financial statements prepared under International Standards, the sections are presented in a different order, but the same information is included on the statement.) In a basic cash system, this will most likely be just your bank accounts. In an accrual system, items you would see in the asset section would be:

- Cash - your business checking account, savings account, and PayPal account.

- Inventory - books you've purchased to take to events to sell or merchandise purchased for sale or to giveaway as swag.

- Prepaid expenses - expenses you've paid for but haven't received the service for, like editor deposits.

- Fixed assets - computer equipment, furniture, and even automobiles purchased for the business that have a long life.

- Accounts receivable - sales you've made but haven't received payment for yet.

Cash

This is an obvious asset. It's the balance in your bank accounts. However, a bank reconciliation needs to be done every month to get an accurate picture of exactly how much cash you have on-hand.

You can't just go by what the bank is showing. It doesn't account for checks or payments you've made that haven't cleared the bank yet, but they reduce your cash on-hand. It also doesn't show any deposits that you've made that haven't posted to your bank account as of the date of the reconciliation, which would increase the amount of cash you have.

PayPal accounts are a type of checking account. You receive funds from other people in it and disburse funds to pay for services or goods. Depending on how much activity goes through your PayPal account, you will also want to reconcile this every month.

Another reason to do regular bank reconciliations is to keep track of payments that haven't cleared in a timely manner. The check could be lost in the mail or the person hasn't cashed it yet for some reason. Knowing this, you can track it down. Also, sometimes duplicate payments are entered into your accounting system in error or put to the wrong account. These errors can be found and fixed while doing a bank reconciliation.

Inventory

This occurs when you purchase a supply of books to sell either on your website or at an event or speaking engagement several months or weeks before the event. These books are considered assets until you sell them. The cost of the books, including shipping, would be categorized as inventory on your balance sheet because they represent an investment in products. If you purchase merchandise to sell, this would also be inventory. When you actually sell the books or products, is when you record the expense.

Prepaid Expenses

Another type of expense that is really an asset you may have is called "prepaid expenses." As the term implies, these are payments for expenses before the service is rendered. These are typically things like:

1. Deposits. When you pay a deposit to your editor to hold your booking of their service, this would be a prepaid expense because they haven't done the editing work yet. This is especially true if it's refundable and something happens and you or the editor decide not to go through with the project.

2. A large block of ISBN numbers. Technically, these are prepaid expenses until you assign the ISBN to a particular book.

3. Insurance. Many times, business insurance is paid for the year in one lump sum or over four or eight payments. This would also be considered a prepaid expense that would be amortized over the policy period.

4. Early registrations. Often you may register months in advance of a writers conference or pay for a booth at an event that is in the future. These would be prepaid and expensed when you attend the conference or event.

5. Book Cover design. Sometimes you will pay for a book cover before the book is written and published. In this case, it technically would be a prepaid expense until you publish the book.

Many businesses have a capitalization policy for prepaid expenses and only record them when they are over a certain amount, typically $300 or $500.

Fixed Assets

This occurs when you purchase assets with a long life like computer equipment or office furniture. These are accounted for as assets and then depreciated over their life, usually three or five years. The monthly depreciation would then be an expense.

Most businesses have a capitalization policy in which purchases like these are only capitalized—counted as assets—when they are over a certain amount, usually $500. If they are under this amount, they are immediately expensed, as the accounting for the depreciation costs more than the asset itself.

Beginning in 2018, in the USA, the tax laws allow you to take a deduction for assets purchased during the year up to $2,000,000. Please consult with a tax accountant for the current allowable amount when you do your taxes. Although this isn't generally accepted accounting practices, many businesses record this as an expense in the year they take the deduction.

Accounts Receivable

If you use the cash-basis method of accounting, you won't have this asset. But if you use the accrual-basis method, you will. Accounts receivable are those monies you've earned from sales—or services rendered—and haven't yet received the payment for them. This would include sales from the various distributors until they remit your royalties. Also, if you do a speaking engagement for an honorarium, and the venue doesn't pay you immediately afterward it would be an accounts receivable.

LIABILITIES - WHAT YOU OWE

The next section on the balance sheet shows what you owe—your liabilities. These are things like loans, credit card balances, deferred revenues, and accounts payable.

Credit Card Balances

If you have and use a business credit card, most likely you will have a balance on it at the end of the month. This balance represents money you owe to the credit card company. Just like bank accounts, credit cards need to be reconciled every month at the statement date to ensure all the expenditures you made are showing up and are accounted for. This is much easier to do if you enter (or have entered for you) your credit card transactions as they occur. Then you can remember what the charge was for. As an added benefit, you won't have your accountant asking, "What did you purchase from so-and-so and what was it for?" when they do the reconciliation. Make sure to get and keep all your credit card receipts until they are entered into your accounting system and the credit card statement has been reconciled.

Loans

There may be times when you need to obtain a loan to fund a large project or expand your business. These would be broken down as short-term loans (less than a year to pay off) or long-term (more than a year). Any payments you make on the loan would be deducted, and any interest accrued on it would be added. This allows you to know exactly how much you owe and to whom at the end of the month.

Deferred Revenue

This isn't a common one, but you may have it in your writing business. Deferred revenue is when you've received money for services or products but haven't performed the service or delivered the product or books. You will have this if you receive a deposit to speak at an event several months in advance. You'd have deferred revenue if you've done pre-sales on your next book on your website, but you haven't published and shipped the book to your customers yet. It could arise if you do a deal for your foreign rights or print rights, and the publisher has paid you an advance. These are liabilities because you owe the person the service or product, or a refund if you don't perform as paid.

Accounts Payable

Like accounts receivable, if you use the cash-basis method of accounting, you won't have this liability. If you use the accrual-basis method, you will. These are the bills for services and products you've purchased that you haven't paid for yet. Many businesses will use the payment of bills as a way to manage their cash flow. They pay only those bills that are due or that they'll receive a discount for paying early and wait to pay the others until they come due.

Sales Tax (or VAT)

If you sell your books on your website, at an event, or sell merchandise, you will need to collect sales tax from your customers and remit it to your state. Until you send the payment to the state, it is a liability. *This is one place you want to keep accurate records of how much you owe.* You don't want to pay significant penalties because you haven't accounted for the sales tax collected properly. When you make a sale that included sales tax, you will record the book price portion to your income and the sales tax portion to the sales tax liability account.

EQUITY OR CAPITAL - WHAT'S LEFT OVER

The last section of the balance sheet is the equity or capital section. It is what's left over from the assets after all the liabilities are paid. The accounting formula for this section is *Assets - Liabilities = Capital or Equity*. A healthy business will reflect a positive equity, while one that is struggling will show a negative equity. Your net income shown on the income statement flows into your equity section of the balance sheet. It either increases your equity when you've had net income or reduces it when you've had a net loss.

SOLE-PROPRIETORSHIP OR PARTNERSHIP

Your equity not only includes the difference between what you own and what you owe, but it also contains the following for a sole-proprietorship or partnership:

Owner/Partner Contributions

These are funds that you've put into the business, either in the form of cash or payments of business expenses from your personal bank accounts or credit cards. This would apply for a sole-proprietorship, partnership, or certain types of LLCs.

Owner/Partner Withdrawals

These are the funds you've pulled out of the business. In the case of a sole-proprietorship or partnership, any monies you pay yourself are a withdrawal and deduction of your equity.

Retained Earnings

This is where the net amount from your income statement flows to your equity, either adding to it or deducting from it. It represents the growth or loss of your business activities. This is usually shown in two amounts:

1. Accumulated income or loss, which represents the earnings of the business since inception through the prior year.
2. Current income or loss, which represents the performance of your business for the current year.

When the company has been profitable, it increases your equity in the business; while when it suffers a loss, you lose equity.

CORPORATION

If you have a corporation, the equity accounts would be presented as follows:

Common Stock

This is reported as the par value of the stock that has been issued to shareholders. For example, if your corporation has a stated par value of $0.01 per common share and has issued 5,000 shares, this value would be $50.00.

If there isn't a stated par value, then the full amount for the purchase of stock would be shown here.

Additional Paid-in Capital

This is the difference between the amount someone has paid for your corporation's stock and the par value. In the above example, the person (you, in a single-shareholder S-Corp) paid $5,000 for the 5,000 shares. The additional paid-in capital amount would be $4,950. In an S-Corporation, this would include any loans given to the company by the shareholder or any assets contributed, such as computers.

Dividends Paid

This would represent the dollar value of any dividends the corporation issued to its shareholders and would be a reduction in the equity amount. There are complicated rules beyond the scope of this book on when and how much a corporation can distribute dividends to its shareholders. This is an issue you need to discuss with a qualified accountant.

Retained Earnings

Retained earnings is the same as detailed above for a sole-proprietorship or partnership.

Chapter 6
Accounting Systems

Accounting Software

You can use any of the accounting software packages like QuickBooks, Xero, or Zoho for your accounting. These can be used whether you choose to use the cash-basis method or the accrual-basis method. Most of these options are cost effective and have a cloud-based system. Using these, if you decide later to work with an accountant, it's a much simpler process (and cost efficient) for them to use the files you already have set up, with minor tweaks. They can also access your books and do your accounting remotely—gotta love technology. Although I believe these programs have applications for outside of the USA, you may need to do a Google search for accounting software in your country.

ACCOUNTANTS

When looking for an accountant, I would recommend first searching for someone who is a financial accountant, then they can recommend you to a tax accountant. The focus of education and expertise is different for each of these types. You will eventually want both. Tax accountants rarely have the expertise needed to help you set up your accounting system and maintain it, or the intricacies involved in various industries. Conversely, financial accountants are good with the books and getting you the data you need for business decisions, but they usually don't do or like taxes; and therefore, aren't up on all the tax law changes.

It certainly helps to work with an accountant who understands the publishing industry and what you need. However, any good financial accountant will have worked with many types of businesses and can tailor your accounting system to fit your business.

(Please note: I am retired from accounting!! I'm now a full-time author with my own writing business. My aim for this book is to help you set up your business and manage it, and the accounting needed, not to gain new clients.)

SIMPLE CASH-BASIS SYSTEM

As mentioned in the section "What to Track and Record Keeping" for a cash-basis accounting system, you can go as simple as a filing system for documents and a spreadsheet to track your income and expenditures. This is essentially an expanded checkbook register you keep on a spreadsheet. You can use Excel, Google sheets, or any other spreadsheet program. Set up a spreadsheet file for the year and have a tab for each month.

When setting up your spreadsheet, think about what your income streams are—or will be. Your spreadsheet will have a column for each of your major ones. Then you'll set up columns for production costs like editing, covers, and proof copies. Then the spreadsheet will have columns for your major marketing expenses and admin expenses. Total each of the columns and each section. To see if you are making a profit or not, subtract your total expenses from your total income. If this number is positive, congratulations! You're making a profit. If it's negative, then your business is losing money.

For the monthly tabs, set up columns for each of your major income and expense categories, plus:

- Date
- Check number, debit card, credit card (indicate how you paid for the item or if it was a deposit)
- Payee or Source (indicate who you paid or where you received the funds from)
- Description (what it was for, especially needed for "Miscellaneous" expenses)
- You'll also need a summary tab to summarize your year-to-date numbers. You'd include each of the income and expense columns from the monthly worksheets, and add the following:
- Month
- Net Profit or (Loss)

An Excel template of this worksheet is included in the sample resource package you can download for free from my website at toramoon.com/bizguide.

BASIC ACCRUAL SYSTEM

To keep your financial books using the accrual-basis method, you will need to use an accounting software package. There are too many pieces to track using just a spreadsheet. These programs, especially the cloud-based ones, are relatively inexpensive and well worth your money. When your business grows where you can hire an accountant to do your books for you, it will be much easier to switch if you're already using an accounting package.

Using accounting software, you can get as granular in collating your data as you'd like. You can have a category of "Book Income," and then have sub-categories like: ebook sales, print sales, audiobook sales. Then you can break it down even further and track for each series you write. If you sell related merchandise, you can have a main category of "Merchandise Income," then break it down into the types of merchandise you sell, like t-shirts, mugs, bags, etc. This way, you can easily tell which series or items are doing well and which ones you may need to scrap or discontinue writing. The same level of detail applies to your production costs and expenses.

CHART OF ACCOUNTS

When setting up an accounting system, it begins with what is called a chart of accounts. This is a list of all the line items that land on your income statement and balance sheet. It's important to enter your data into the correct accounts so that your financial statements are correct and reflect an accurate picture of your business' health.

Remember, these documents summarize your business activity data. Think about how detailed you want your information and what income and expense items are important to you to track, monitor, and manage. You can always add accounts or detail as you go. If you didn't think of an expense when you set up your system, but find you have a lot of expenditures for it, you can add it, and it will flow into your financial statements.

As part of the chart of accounts, each line item in the chart is assigned to an account type. These tell the accounting system where it flows to on your financial statements. If the chart of accounts isn't set up correctly, your financial statements and other documents won't be correct either. Because it is so important, I have included a comprehensive sample chart of accounts in the sample package that you can use. It is specific to a writing business' needs. I use this chart of accounts for my writing business. Getting this set up right at the beginning will ensure your system will work the way it's supposed to and give you the data and information you need.

One of the major differences in using an accrual system rather than cash-basis is that in an accrual system, you are recording your sales in the month they occur. This creates a receivable account, which is an asset and is shown on your balance sheet. When you receive payment from the distributor, this receivable amount is reduced, and your cash is increased.

Another difference is that expenses are recorded in the period they apply to rather than when you pay them. This can occur when you prepay an expense, like registering for a writer's conference in January, but it isn't held until October. This creates a prepaid expense—or an asset. Or it can happen when the service was rendered, but you don't pay the bill for another month or two. An example of this would be receiving an invoice from your editor in May, but you don't pay it until the middle of June. This would be called an accounts payable—or a liability.

In the sample "Income Statement" and "Balance Sheet," I have included one using the accrual method and one using the cash-basis method for you to see the differences.

Chapter 7
Analyzing Your Business

Metrics

Your business generates a lot of data that is useful to managing your business and making business decisions. Your accounting system is one place, but there are other metrics you may want to use to analyze your business. If you haven't yet, I suggest you make spreadsheets your friends. They make analysis much easier than pencil and paper.

Metrics are those things that you can measure and have set milestones for. These will tell you if you are hitting the goals you have set for yourself and your business. If they haven't been met, then you need to look at the underlying cause to determine what needs to be fixed, tweaked, revised, or even scrapped. Although metrics can be anything that can be measured, they have to have meaning for you and your business.

Examples of helpful metrics for analyzing your business are:

- Book Sales. Number and amount sold from each distributor and retailer. You may want to break this down further into geographic locations, and segregate it between ebook sales, print sales, and audiobook sales.

- Direct Sales: Sales directly from your website or at events. You may want to track the number of books sold, which books (title), and the type (ebook or print), and the type of event, etc.

- If you're in the Kindle Select program, you may want to track the number of page reads for each book in the program and by geographic location.

- Marketing campaigns: Calculate the return on investment (ROI) for each campaign, including read-through rates. (Brian Meeks' book, *Mastering Amazon Ads*, and Mal Cooper's book, *Help! My Facebook Ads Suck* both go into this in great detail, as does Mark Dawson's *Ads for Authors* course.)

- Read-through rates: The number of books in the series that are sold after book one and the ratio. (The above referenced books and course also go into this in great detail).

- Break-even point for your monthly expenses and for each book. See the section "Break-Even Point" for details on how to calculate this.

- Mailing List: Number of subscribers month over month, how engaged your subscribers are, and which links or type of links are clicked.

- Number of books given away in each cross-promotion you participate in or other giveaways.

- Number of reviews.
- Number of books or series you've written, or publications your work is in (for short stories, poems, articles, etc.).
- Number of events spoken at or attended. You may want to include the number of books sold at each event.

BREAK-EVEN POINT

You may want to calculate your break-even point, whether for your business as a whole or for an individual book or series. A break-even point is the tipping point from going from non-profitable to profitable. This occurs when all of your direct expenses are met by your sales.

To calculate the monthly break-even point for your business, total all the fixed expenses you will have every month whether you make any sales or not. This would include costs such as: email provider, BookFunnel fees, software subscriptions, cell phone charges, rent (if you rent an office), and internet access fees. If you have employees, add in their gross pay. This total represents how much you have to make each month to be profitable.

Next, divide this total by the average NET selling price of your books. The resulting calculation will be how many books you have to sell each month in order to cover your fixed costs. You don't want to use the selling price of your books because you don't receive the full amount. Use the amount you actually receive from Amazon and the other distributors. If you have more than one book, use the average net revenues you receive over all your books, and across all the distributors.

For example: My average net revenue over all my books, from all distributors, is $2.45. (This also takes into account foreign exchange rates.) I calculated a fixed monthly cost of $225. I have to sell 92 books per month in order to cover my monthly costs. This is after the books have recovered their production costs.

Monthly Expense	Cost
MailerLite	25
Bookfunnel	20
Prolific Works	15
ReaderLinks	10
Cellphone	75
Internet	70
Research Materials	10
Total Fixed Costs	225
Ave Net Rev of All Books (Divide)	2
Number of Books to Cover Costs	92

You can use this calculation for your budgeting. Add up the fixed expenses you have every month, add in a budgeted amount for marketing and your desired monthly profit, then divide by the average net revenue for your books. This will give you how many books you need to sell each month to cover your costs and make a living.

For example: Taking the above $225 for fixed monthly expenses and adding in a $500 budget for marketing expenses, and $2,500 in living expenses (profit), totals $3,225. Using the same average net revenue for all my books, from all distributors, of $2.45, I need to sell an average of 1,316 books per month.

Monthly Expenses	Cost
Fixed Costs	225
Advertising	500
Profit (Salary)	2,500
Total Monthly Amount	3,225
Ave Net Rev of All Books (Divide)	2
Number of Books to Cover Costs	1,316

To calculate this for a book, you will need to gather all the costs associated with producing the book. This will be the editing, cover design, formatting, printing, and other costs you incurred to get it ready for production. Total these costs, then divide them with the NET selling price of the book. Don't use the retail price of the book, but the net royalty you will receive from the distributors for the book. This will give you the number of books you need to sell just to pay for the cost of producing it. Once this number is reached, any additional books you sell is profit.

For example, for my book Exile's Vengeance, it cost me $1,945 in editing and $230 for the cover, for a total production cost of $2,175. The selling price for this book is $4.99, but I don't receive the full selling price. My net from Amazon, after distribution fees, is $3.40 per book. I divided the costs of $2,175 by $3.40, which equals 640. I need to sell 640 books to recover my production costs.

Production Expenses	Cost
Editing	1,945
Cover	230
Total Cost for Book	2,175
Net Rev of Book (Divide)	3
Number of Books to Cover Costs	640

A template for calculating your break-even point is included in the sample package found on my website.

Chapter 8
Samples & Resources

The following sample condensed financial statements were prepared using the accrual-basis and cash-basis method of accounting for a fictional Indie publishing company. The same data was used for both types of statements to show you the differences in each method.

I've included a copy of these sample financial statements along with other templates you can use for your business. These are available to download for free from my website at: toramoon.com/bizguide.

CHAPTER 8: SAMPLES & RESOURCES

The Sample Package includes:

Sample Financial statements, these show more line items.

- Sample Balance Sheet, accrual-basis
- Sample Income Statement, accrual-basis
- Sample Balance Sheet, cash-basis
- Sample Income Statement, cash-basis

Templates and Other Information:

- Chart of Accounts, with an explanation for each account
- Excel template for Simple Cash-Basis accounting system
- Excel template for calculating your break-even point
- Instructions on filling out a Form SS-4 to receive an EIN from the IRS

SAMPLE PUBLISHING COMPANY
Balance Sheet
As of Dec. 31, 20xx
(Accrual Basis)

ASSETS

Cash	$35,595
Accounts Receivable	2,579
Inventory	2,605
Prepaid Expenses	4,055
Total Assets	**$44,834**

LIABILITIES AND EQUITY
LIABILITIES:

Accounts Payable	$525
Credit Card Payable	4,275
Sales Tax Liability	150
Total Liabilities	4,950

EQUITY:

Owner's Equity	20,006
Accumulated Net Income/(Loss)	(6,417)
Current Year Net Income	26,295
Total Equity	39,884
Total Liab & Equity	**$44,834**

SAMPLE PUBLISHING COMPANY
Income Statement
For the Year Ended Dec. 31, 20xx
(Accrual Basis)

REVENUES

Book Sales	$45,720
Speaking Honorariums	2,500
Teaching Fees	4,500
Merchandise Sales	2,300
TOTAL REVENUES	55,020
TOTAL COST OF SALES:	9,700
GROSS PROFIT	**45,320**

EXPENSES

Marketing and Sales Expenses	6,370
General & Admin Expenses:	12,840
Total Operating Expenses	19,210
Net Operating Income/(Loss)	26,110

Other Income/(Expense):	
Affiliate Income	545
Interest Expense	(360)
Total Other Income/(Expense)	185
NET INCOME/(LOSS)	**$26,295**

SAMPLE PUBLISHING COMPANY
Balance Sheet
As of Dec. 31, 20xx
(Cash Basis)

ASSETS

Checking	$35,595
Total Assets	**35,595**

LIABILITIES AND EQUITY

LIABILITIES

Credit Card Payable	4,275
Sales Tax Liability	150
Total Liabilities	**4,425**

EQUITY

Owner's Equity	20,006
Accumulated Net Income/(Loss)	(6,417)
Current Year Net Income	17,581
Total Equity	31,170
Total Liababilities and Equity	**$35,595**

SAMPLE PUBLISHING COMPANY
Income Statement
For the Year Ended Dec. 31, 20xx
(Cash Basis)

REVENUES

Book Sales	$43,140
Other Revenues	9,300
TOTAL REVENUES	52,440
COST OF SALES	15,830
GROSS PROFIT	**36,610**

EXPENSES

Marketing and Sales Expenses	6,370
General & Admin Expenses:	12,840
Total Operating Expenses	19,210
Net Operating Income/(Loss)	17,400

Other Income/(Expense):

Affiliate Income	545
Interest Expense	(364)
Total Other Income/(Expense)	181
NET INCOME/(LOSS)	**$17,581**

HELPFUL LINKS

Below are helpful links in setting up and running your writing and publishing business. I have personally used or looked into each of these products. They may, or may not, work for your business but they're worth looking into and making that decision for yourself. I'm not receiving an affiliate commission for any of these sources. They may have changed since this book was published. You may download a pdf of this list with the links from my website at: toramoon.com/bizguide

Setting Up and Legal

Every state has information on how to set up and register a business in the state. Search for your state, but be sure the extension is .gov to ensure you are on the state's official website.

Applying for an EIN (Form SS-4): www.irs.gov/businesses/small-businesses-self-employed/employer-id-numbers

Trademark search: www.uspto.gov/trademarks-application-process/search-trademark-database

Obtaining ISBNs in the U.S.A.: www.myidentifiers.com

Reedsy Article on ISBNs: blog.reedsy.com/how-to-get-an-isbn

U.S. Sales Tax Articles from Avalara

U.S. Sales Tax Nexus Article: www.avalara.com/us/en/learn/ guides/sales-tax-101/chapter-4-nexus-and-sales-tax-laws.html This provides a good explanation, with links, of what the different states consider for nexus and the limitations.

U.S. Sales Tax Economic Nexus Article (as of 2021): www.avalara. com/us/en/learn/guides/sales-tax-nexus-laws-by-state.html

Summary of each state's requirements (as of May 2019): www. avalara.com/us/en/learn/guides/state-by-state-guide-economic-nexus-laws.html Please check with the individual states for updated information as tax laws change constantly.

Distributing Your Books

The book, Wide for the Win, goes into detail on how to distribute and upload your books to the various distributors.

Amazon KDP: kdp.amazon.com (this is for the US site)

Kobo: writinglife.kobo.com

Apple: authors.apple.com

Barnes & Noble: press.barnesandnoble.com

Google Play: play.google.com/store

Findaway Voices (Audiobooks): findawayvoices.com

IngramSpark (print): ingramspark.com

Aggregators

Draft2Digital: www.draft2digital.com/ (I use Draft2Digital and found it easy to use and they have some other great tools like a universal book link.)

Smashwords: www.smashwords.com/ (I haven't used Smashwords. They were the first in this space and are well-respected.)

PublishDrive: publishdrive.com

Amazon Information

Amazon digital pricing requirements: kdp.amazon.com/en_US/help/topic/G200634500

Amazon 70% royalty price requirements: kdp.amazon.com/en_US/help/topic/G200634560

Ebook Author Cross-Promotion Sites

BookFunnel: bookfunnel.com/

Prolific Works: www.prolificworks.com/authors

Story Origin: storyoriginapp.com/

Tools for Keywords

Publisher Rocket: publisherrocket.com/ helps you find and compile keyword lists for AMS advertising. It's sold through Kindlepreneur

Google Adwords Planner. You need a Google ad account to search for these. It's free but you will have to set up an ad and pause it to get to the ad planner.

Other Useful Links

Self-Publishing Formula: selfpublishingformula.com Both Mark Dawson's SPF 101 and Ads for Authors courses are excellent. He also has a very good podcast series.

Kindlepreneur: kindlepreneur.com He has good Indie Publishing information for both fiction and nonfiction. He also has a list of promo sites kindlepreneur.com/list-sites-promote-free-amazon-books

The Book Designer: A website by Joel Friedlander with scads of articles and resources for designing and publishing your book. Unfortunately, with Mr. Friedlander's death, the last book cover design award was in 2020. The archived awards are helpful for researching what makes a good cover design. www.thebookdesigner.com/category/cover-design

TV Tropes: A good website to research the various tropes for both TV and fiction. tvtropes.org/pmwiki/pmwiki.php/Main/Tropes

Article on indie publishing tax issues in the UK: www.hwfisher.co.uk/wp-content/uploads/2018/06/2Authors-and-Journalists_Tax-guide_A5-SINGLE-PAGE-SPREAD.pdf

Alliance for Independent Authors (Alli) is a great organization which works for strengthening the Indie Author community. They have a great blog. selfpublishingadvice.org/

Podcasts

The Self-Publishing Show (Mark Dawson and James Blatch)

The Creative Penn (JoAnna Penn)

Six-Figure Authors (Lindsay Buroker, Andrea Pearson, and Joseph R. Lallo)

Facebook Groups

Wide for the Win. A great group for all things of going and being "wide." www.facebook.com/groups/wideforthewin

20Books to 50K. A group for the business of being an indie publisher. They produce an amazing writer's conference every November in Las Vegas, USA. www.facebook.com/groups/781495321956934

SPF Community (Mark Dawson's Self-Publishing Formula group): www.facebook.com/groups/1584291371854759

WRITING TOOLS

These are the writing tools I use that I've found very helpful. None of these are affiliate links.

Scrivener: A word processing program developed for writers. I use it not only for my books, but for my newsletter and social media. I've also used it to create courses. Anything I'm writing that needs organization is done in Scrivener. It's available for MAC and PC at an extremely affordable price. www.literatureandlatte.com/scrivener/overview

Trello: Kanban-style web-based list making app. Great for production plans. trello.com

Grammar Software: I prefer using ProWritingAid. Like all AI based programs, you do need to access the suggestions and determine if it's right for your book. For instance, I rarely use their "readability enhancement" suggestions as they aren't how people write or speak. I don't use all the functions. I love the "echoes" function; it's helped me tighten up my writing. Grammarly is a similar program, I just liked ProWritingAid better for my writing when I tested them.

ProWritingAid: prowritingaid.com

Grammerly: www.grammarly.com

Reading Resources

General Indie Publishing and Business

Indie Author Guide: Author Business Plan Workbook by Tora Moon

Business for Authors: How to be an Autherpreneur by Joanna Penn

Wide for the Win by Mark Leslie Lefebvre

The Relaxed Author by Joanna Penn and Mark Leslie Lefebvre

Indie Author Survival Guide by S.K. Quinn

Write, Publish, Repeat by Sean Platt & Johnny B. Truant

Let's Get Digital by David Gaughran

Self-Publisher's Legal Handbook: Updated Guide to Protecting Your Rights and Wallet by Helen Sedwick

The Author's Guide to Cover Design by Stuart Bache

Self-Publish Strong Books 1-4: The Complete How-To Guide for Building a Rock-Solid Platform, Accelerating Your Author Brand, and Creating a Successful Newsletter List by Andrea Pearson

Become a Successful Indie Author: Work Toward Your Writing Dream by Craig Martelle

Release Strategies: Plan Your Self-Publishing Schedule for Maximum Benefit by Craig Martelle

Newsletter Ninja: How to Become an Author Mailing List Expert by Tammi Labrecque

Audio for Authors: Audiobooks, Podcasting, and Voice Technologies by Joanna Penn

Marketing, Ads, and Cover Copy (blurb)

How to Market a Book by Joanna Penn

Mastering Amazon Ads: An Authors Guide by Brian Meeks

Mastering Simple Facebook Ads for Authors by Mark J Dawson and Kerry Gardiner

Help! My Facebook Ads Suck: Simple Steps to Turn Those Ads Around by Mal Cooper

Help! My Blurbs and Ad Copy Suck: Learn an Easy and Fun Process for Writing Blurbs and Ad Copy by Mal Cooper

Writing Killer Cover Copy by Elana Johnson

Get Your Book Selling Wide by Monica Leonelle

Six Figure Author: Using Data to Sell Books by Chris Fox

Write to Market: Deliver a Book that Sells by Chris Fox

How to Write a Sizzling Synopsis: A Step-by-Step System for Enticing New Readers, Selling More Fiction, and Making Your Book Sound Good by Bryan Cohen

Gotta Read It! Five Simple Steps to a Fiction Pitch That Sells by Libbie Hawker

How to Write Fiction Sales Copy by Dean Wesley Smith

Writing Craft

Emotional Thesaurus by Angela Ackerman

She Sat He Stood: What Do Your Characters Do While They Talk? By Ginger Hanson

2K to 10K: How to Write Faster, Write Better, and Write More of What You Love by Rachel Aaron

The Heroine's Journey: For Writers, Readers, and Fans of Pop Culture by Gail Carriger

Million Dollar Productivity by Kevin J. Anderson

Self-Editing

The Novel Editing Workbook by Kris Spisak

Self-Editing for Fiction Writers by Renni Browne

Next Steps

There's so much to consider and do when creating and growing a business. This book has talked about the basics of setting up and managing your author business. Creating a business plan can give you the roadmap of where you want your business to be in the next year or more. I've written a companion book to help you create your business plan, Business Plan for Authors.

The Business Plan for Authors and the accompanying workbook will guide you through the process of creating your author business plan. Each section includes questions to consider for your business and checklists to track your decisions. By the end of the book, you'll have a fully developed plan for your author business.

Get your copy today!

More resources and information is available on my website:
ToraMoon.com/IndieGuides

**Signup to receive updates on new books
in the Indie Author Guide Series**

ALSO BY TORA MOON

Indie Author Guides

Business and Accounting for Authors
Author Business Plan Workbook

Legends of Lairheim (Science-Fantasy)

Ancient Enemies
Ancient Allies
The Scourge Incursion
Exile's Vengeance
Redemption

The Sentinel Witches (Urban Fantasy)

Crossroads to Destiny
Descent Into Darkness
Well of Sorrows

Visit www.ToraMoon.com
To get an up-to-date listing of all my books
You can find these titles at your favorite retail store, on
my website, or ask your library to order them for you.

ABOUT THE AUTHOR

Tora Moon writes genre-bending fantasy and science fiction. She loves blending elements from various genres. Common elements that seem to show up in all her stories is a Goddess, shapeshifters, and magic. There is also usually a romantic sub-plot because love is an important part of life.

Before turning to writing full-time, Tora was a Certified Public Accountant (CPA) for over twenty-years, specializing in working with small businesses clients, setting up their accounting systems, doing their accounting, and preparing their financial statements. She has worked with small publicly-traded companies doing their accounting, working with their financial auditors, and preparing and filing their quarterly and annual financial statements with the U.S. Securities and Exchange Commission (SEC). For three years, she served as the Chief Financial Officer (CFO) for a publicly-traded software development firm with operations in four different countries and listed on two different stock exchanges.

Besides reading, some of her hobbies are sewing, crocheting, and making wire wrapped jewelry. Her love of travel has taken her to several countries and saw her living in an RV for several years. She makes her home in the southwestern desert with her feline companion.

You can find out more about her and her
work at www.toramoon.com

Thank You!

I hope this book has helped you in treating your writing as a business, setting it up, and the importance of tracking and managing your money. Don't forget to download your free Sample and Resources Package at: **toramooncom/bizguide.**

The companion book, Author Business Plan Workbook, takes you through the steps to create a business plan for your author business.

If you've found value in this book, please help other authors find this book by leaving a review on the retail site where you purchased this book, review it on a blog, or even just tell your friends about it.

The truth is, VERY few readers leave reviews. Please help me by being the exception.

I love hearing from my readers!

Follow my author page on Facebook (Tora Moon, Author)
Visit my website (www.toramoon.com)
Email me (tora@toramoon.com)

Made in United States
North Haven, CT
02 December 2023

44896602R00075